Social Equity and Public Administration

Social Equity and Public Administration

Origins, Developments, and Applications

H. George Frederickson

M.E.Sharpe
Armonk, New York
London, England

Library of Congress Cataloging-in-Publication Data

Frederickson, H. George.
  Social equity and public administration : origins, developments, and applications /
by H. George Frederickson.
     p. cm.
  Includes bibliographical references and index.
  ISBN 978-0-7656-2471-0 (cloth : alk. paper) — 978-0-7656-2472-7 (pbk. : alk. paper)
    1. Public administration. 2. Public welfare—Management. I. Title.

JF1351.F7345 2010
351—dc22   2009030627

Printed in the United States of America

The paper used in this publication meets the minimum requirements of
American National Standard for Information Sciences
Permanence of Paper for Printed Library Materials,
ANSI Z 39.48-1984.

∞

CW (c) 10   9   8   7   6   5   4   3   2   1
CW (p) 10   9   8   7   6   5   4   3   2   1

To the memory of
Stewart Lofgren Grow
1913–1983

Contents

Preface

In the mid-1990s, Phil Rutledge and I first started talking about bringing together my essays on social equity in public administration. At the time, we were working together on the charter for what would become the Standing Panel on Social Equity in Governance of the National Academy of Public Administration. Phil pointed out that my work on social equity was scattered about in books, journals, lectures, and papers, some of it in rather fugitive places. He also pointed out that I might have a singular sense of the origins and evolution of social equity in public administration, that a collection of my writings on social equity in a single publication might be useful to future teachers and practitioners of public administration, and that I was not getting any younger. Despite Phil's urgings, in the years that followed, I continued to write contemporary essays on social equity, managing to stay abreast of the subject while putting off the publication of a collection.

For the past decade, I have been working with Harry Briggs, executive editor at M.E. Sharpe Inc., on several book projects. In all of these projects, he has demonstrated that mix of professionalism, enthusiasm, and high standards that fills authors with confidence and trust. After Phil Rutledge died, in 2007, and feeling badly that I had not put together the collection that he had recommended, I approached Harry with the idea. With his usual enthusiasm, we began with an outline and an agreement, and I went to work.

My assistant, Katherine Logan, has cheerfully labored through countless drafts, bringing the keen eye of an English major to the task. I thank her.

Many years ago, while an undergraduate at Brigham Young University, I majored in political science. While politics was interesting, it was not for me. I nevertheless wished to be engaged in government. Then I enrolled in my first public administration course. It was taught by Stewart Grow, an exciting and powerful professor. When the course was complete, thanks to Professor Grow, I knew exactly what was interesting to me and what I would do. I also knew that public administration was important, that part of government where a person like me might make a difference. This book is dedicated to him.

Introduction

There have been many indicators over the past decade that social equity is now a core topic in public administration and public policy. For example, in 1997 the congressionally chartered National Academy of Public Administration established a Standing Panel on Social Equity. One of only four, the panel was established to be a forum for the deliberation of fellows of the academy on matter of fairness, justice, and equity in public administration practice and theory. In addition, the new standing panel was charged with being a voice for social equity values in all of the work of the academy including funded academy studies of particular public administration problems and challenges. In the past ten years, the Standing Panel on Social Equity has convened annual conferences, held well-attended monthly luncheon meetings, and issued sundry reports and publications. It is now generally agreed that this panel is the largest and most active standing panel in the academy. Social equity is an idea whose time has clearly come to the National Academy of Public Administration.

With a grant from James Nordin, the American Society for Public Administration (ASPA) established the Gloria Hobson Nordin Social Equity Award in 2002. Given annually, the Nordin Award "recognizes lifetime achievement and effort in the cause of social equity . . . in the public sector." The award is given at the Social Equity Plenary Luncheon held at the annual ASPA conference. In addition to the Nordin award and luncheon, the annual ASPA conferences now include many panels and papers on various aspects of social equity. At the 2009 ASPA conference in Miami, for example, there were thirteen panels with forty papers on many aspects of the subject.

The National Association of Schools of Public Affairs and Administration (NASPAA) is the home of the Commission on Peer Review and Accrediting (COMPRA) in public administration and policy. COMPRA sets the standards and requirements for the professional masters degree in public administration, the MPA (there are variations in degree nomenclature, depending on the university granting the degree, but the MPA is by far the most common designation). To be an accredited degree, an MPA curriculum must include several core subjects such as management and leadership, critical thinking,

and analysis. In the late 1990s, these phrases were added to the core requirements: "to incorporate into decisions of considerations of ethics, fiscal and
environmental sustainability and social equity. To communicate and interact
productively with a diverse and changing workforce and citizenry."

These and many other clues, signs, and signals mark the growing importance of social equity in public administration and policy. As a primary
subject in the field, social equity has a unique and identifiable origin and an
interesting provenance. The purpose of this book is to describe the origins of
social equity in public administration and its emergence as one of the central
principles in the field.

Although unaware of it at the time, I started writing this book forty years
ago. It began as a chapter in another book (Marini 1971), and evolved to
serve as the foundation upon which a slow but steady social equity perspective on public policy and administration has been built. Rather than springing
full grown into theory and practice, the social equity perspective on public
policy and administration grew and evolved. Other perspectives on public
administration, the reinventing government movement, for example, have
been better known and noisier. And others, the market model, for example,
have been imported to public administration from other fields, particularly
economics. The social equity perspective grew from within, in the body of
public administration. It was Dwight Waldo who first described the influence
of social equity on the body of public administration as a ductless gland, a
subtle but important influence on the field.

Social Equity could be described as a variation on traditional approaches to
the history of ideas. The book does not attempt to prove anything. Nor does
it make propositions or claims that rise to the level of formal social science.
In view of the excessive "scientific" and "empirical' claims of some social
science, I make no apologies for this. Instead, *Social Equity* is a loose phenomenology of the place of social equity in the development and evolution of
the fields of public policy and administration. It reaches for explanations of
the place of fairness, justice, and equality in the theory and practice of public
policy and administration. And it reaches for explanations of the influence
of events on the theory and practice of social equity, how social equity may
have influenced the perceptions of events and shaped responses to them. With
respect to matters of fairness, justice, and equality *Social Equity* attempts to
account for how public policy and administration has come to be as it is.

My primary purpose, however, is not historical. History is a useful vehicle
for the description of the development of an idea over time and for the interaction between that idea and the sequence of events in time. The emergence of
social equity as a perspective on public policy and administration is framed
in time, and the shifting context in which that perspective has been played

out is important. Nevertheless, it is the idea of social equity that matters most. Context merely helps to explain its development as an idea and particularly the nuances of that idea.

Still, we start with history.

Forty years ago, the United States was bogged down in an unpopular war, the war in Vietnam. Unlike the relatively civil response to the war in Iraq by those opposed to it, the public response to the war in Vietnam was big, loud, angry, and persistent. Campus buildings were occupied, and some were set on fire; universities were closed; some students were shot and killed; mothers protested daily on the steps of courthouses across the land; and leading journalists and television news anchors spoke openly against the war. Among the many points raised by these protesters was that the *administration* of the war in Vietnam was unfair.

The war in Vietnam was nested in the wider context of the earlier assassinations of President John F. Kennedy, the Reverend Martin Luther King, and Senator Robert Kennedy. Urban riots and destruction were widespread. Dwight Waldo later referred to the period as a time of turbulence. He had attended a conference of leading public administration scholars and practitioners in Philadelphia in 1967 and came away surprised that the conference did not include anyone under age fifty. He was further surprised that the content of the conference had little connection to the pressing issues of the day. In discussing this with his colleagues at the Maxwell School of Citizenship and Public Affairs at Syracuse University, he wondered aloud whether younger people in public administration had perspectives on the field that were more relevant to the turbulent times. To test this proposition, he hit on the idea of a small conference limited to young public administration specialists, young defined as less than thirty-five years of age. He commissioned three of his junior colleagues, H. George Frederickson, Harry Lambright, and Frank Marini, to plan, organize, and operate the conference. In anticipation of a book of conference proceedings, twelve participants were invited to write papers in advance, and three, the conference organizers, agreed to write papers afterward summarizing conference themes and perspectives. The gathering was held in early September 1968 at the Minnowbrook Conference Center of Syracuse University on Blue Mountain Lake in the Adirondack Mountains of New York.

If coverage on Google and Wikipedia are marks of status, the Minnowbrook Conference is iconic. As a broadly based critique of public administration, the Minnowbrook perspective is an enduring legend, with its own narrative and attendant mystique and mythology (Marini 1971; Waldo 1971; Frederickson 1980). This meeting is now known as Minnowbrook I; there have been two subsequent conferences, Minnowbrook II in 1988 and Minnowbrook III in 2008. The Minnowbrook conferences are the cicadas of public administration—appearing every twenty years to make a lot of noise then slipping back into the earth to rest and prepare for their next appearance. And so it is that every public administration generation has its own Minnowbrook, its own critique of public administration.

At the first Minnowbrook, I was struck by the persistence of issues of fairness, justice, and equality in the papers and discourse. The issues of the day—the war in Vietnam, urban riots, campus disruption, social protest—were freighted with questions of fairness, justice, and equality. The primary themes of the conference were:

- The relevance of public administration to the issues of the day
- The democratic grounding of public administration
- Public administration as a moral enterprise
- Internal democratic administration
- Fairness, justice, and equality in public administration

Having agreed to write a book chapter summarizing and synthesizing one or more of the conference themes, I set to work. From the outset, it was evident that issues of fairness, justice, and equality in public administration permeated the other four themes. It was also clear that the social equity issues needed to be uncoupled from the other conference themes and given separate treatment. Finally, the phrase "fairness, justice, and equality" was cumbersome. A shorter and simpler expression would help. At an early stage of research on the subject, I began to use the phrase "social equity" as shorthand for the longer phrase, and over time it stuck.

The only extensive literature on the subject was found in administrative law, a literature on justice from the public administration perspective. Although it was clear that administrative law was very important, the legal perspective on social equity did not seem adequate. Laws and regulations often describe what should not be done and set the vital boundaries around the range of administrative discretion. Laws spell out and affirm individual and group rights. But laws and regulations are often ineffective guides for administrators trying to determine what to do. However trite this observation may seem, laws and regulations are better at telling administrators what not to do than what to do.

A comprehensive review of the public administration literature found virtually no treatment of fairness and equality, the other aspects of social equity that seemed so pervasive at Minnowbrook I. So, it was necessary to build the social equity perspective on public administration from scratch. Chapter 1 is that essay, the original description of social equity in public administration, the first attempt to create that perspective.

The chapter situates social equity as one of the three primary general purposes of public administration—the *efficient, economical,* and *equitable* organization and management of public services. Social equity is now often referred to as the "third pillar" in public administration, after efficiency and economy. All three pillars are in fact expressions of values and preferences. In fairly strict terms, efficiency values have to do with achieving the most, the best, or the most preferable public services for available resources. Efficiency asks this question: under the circumstances are public services being organized and delivered as well as possible? In strict terms, economy values in public administration have to do with the management of scarce resources and particularly with expending the fewest resources for an agreed-upon level of public services. Economy asks this question: what is the least we can spend under the circumstances?

Social equity values have to do with the fairness of the organization, its management, and its delivery of public services. Social equity asks these questions: For whom is the organization well managed? For whom is the organization efficient? For whom is the organization economical? For whom are public services more or less fairly delivered?

Considerations of efficiency and economy in public administration tend to assume a kind of "oneness" to the public, an assumption that may be helpful analytically. In the pursuit of efficiency, public officials will strive to make the entire organization and its delivery of public services efficient or economical, assuming that all of the public served by the organization will benefit, more or less in equal measure, from greater efficiency or economy. It is clearly evident that the public is highly varied—rich and poor, old and young, fortunate and unfortunate, urban and suburban—and that while public services may, in a general sense, be more efficient or economical, in the specific sense, these public services will almost certainly be efficient and economical for some more than for others. And so, the values of efficiency, economy, *and* social equity are essential to both the theory and practice of public administration.

What, in more precise terms, are social equity values? For the broadest definition, one can turn to *Black's Law Dictionary* (1957): "[Equity] denotes the spirit and the habit of fairness and justice and right dealing which would regulate the intercourse of men . . . its obligation is ethical rather than jural, and its discussion belongs to the sphere of morals."

The philosopher John Rawls states: "For us the primary subject of justice is the basic structure of society, or more exactly, the way in which major social institutions distribute fundamental rights and duties and determine the division of advantages from social cooperation. By major institutions I understand the political constitution and the principle economic and social arrangements" (1971, 7).

Furthermore, according to Rawls, each person possesses an inviolability founded on the justice that even the welfare of society as a whole cannot override. In a just society the liberties of equal citizenship are taken as settled; the rights secured by justice are not subject to political bargaining or to the calculus of social interest (1971, 3–4).

The Rawlsian claim that fairness and justice are among the rights of citizenship informs the arguments in chapter 1. These arguments have a distinct advocacy tone to them, calling for a view of public administration that not only is not neutral as regards fairness and justice, but is also committed to their pursuit. A forthright and open challenge to the long-standing public administration premise of neutrality was novel in 1968. To assert that public administrators should be anything but neutral, indeed that they should be dedicated to the particular purposes of their agencies—the military for national defense, principals and superintendents for public education—may now seem obvious. Furthermore, public administration should be dedicated to the setting of fair and just policies guiding their agencies and to the fair and just implementation of those policies. This is not to suggest that public administrators should be partisan or engaged in electoral politics. At the time, these were brazen ideas (V.A. Thompson 1975). The emergence of the public policy schools in the 1970s and 1980s, with their rather forthright engagement in policy matters in the name of policy leadership, to get public policy out from under "the dead hand of social science" (a popular phrase at the time) greatly weakened the defense of claims for bureaucratic neutrality. With the passage of time, the advocacy of a public administration that is committed both to their policy purposes and to the fair and just administration of those purposes has become far less controversial.

Absent an overall claim of neutrality, public policy and administration found it necessary to fall back and regroup. The fallback was to a more open consideration of values and norms in the field and particularly to values and norms in the context of alternative theories or models of public policy and administration. Chapter 2, "Social Equity in Context," is an elaboration of the values and norms of public policy and administration in multi-theoretical and multidisciplinary contexts. This elaboration is an early and primitive presentation of a contemporary multi-theoretical and multidisciplinary approach to public administration that eventually formed the framework for *The Public Administration Theory Primer* published in 2003 (Frederickson and Smith). The chapter starts with political science, the political context of public policy and administration, and the primacy of democratic values; it then presents five models or theories of public policy and administration, their early leading theorists, their empirical foci, their characteristics, and the values they tend to maximize. These models—the bureaucratic model, the neobureaucratic model, the institutional model, the human relations model, and the public choice model—are now more or less standard in the field of public administration. Unique here is the particular attention to norms and values—responsiveness, worker and citizen participation, social equity, citizen choice, and administrative responsibility for program effectiveness—and the optimal organizational and managerial means by which these can be furthered. The multi-theoretical and multidisciplinary consideration of norms and values in public policy and administration are finally connected to John Rawls's theoretical construct of fairness as justice (1971).

Chapter 3 touches on considerations of questions of social equity in early American political development and, using this foundation, turns to defining the social equity problem. Using the "social equity as the third pillar of public administration" claim, chapter 3 describes the response to that claim in the evolving literature of the field. Building on this foundation chapter 3 then turns to the descriptive task of setting out some of the complexities and nuances of the subject in the language of a "compound theory of social equity." The point is that the ideas, concepts, and claims that are brought together under the phrase "social equity" are at least as complex and difficult as the ideas, concepts, and claims that make up the efficiency and economy pillars of public administration.

If there is a staple framing of the question of what ought to be the range of administrative discretion, it would be the debate between Friedrich (1940) and Finer (1941). The social equity perspective is distinctly in the Friedrich camp. In short, it is logically impossible to defend social equity without defending the legitimacy of administrative discretion. Chapter 4 is that defense. It begins with the disagreement between Plato and Aristotle over the role of judges and then turns to the arguments of the modern Aristotelian Ronald Dworken. From there chapter 4 deals more directly with contemporary public policy and administration and the neo-Platonists Theodore Lowi and Judith Gruber; it then turns to contemporary public administration theory and the modern works of Dwight Waldo and David Rosenbloom, theorists who approach public administration and policy from the perspective of democratic political philosophy. Recognizing that public administration is a multidisciplinary field, chapter 4 closes with an argument from social psychology that the actual "street level" practices of fairness, justice, and equity inside public agencies provide much of the social glue upon which effective performance is based, and likewise, in the delivery of public services, one finds the taproot of democratic legitimacy.

Closing the first half of *Social Equity*, chapter 5 is an early twenty-first-century summing-up of the status of forty years of the practices of social equity in public administration. The claim is made that there has been considerable social equity progress both in the academic-philosophical and educational sense, and in the applied and practical sense. But the 1990s were not good for the practice of social equity, and chapter 5 is a call to regroup, which is more fully elaborated in a virtual conversation with Philip J. Rutledge in chapter 9.

The careful reader will have noted that the first half of *Social Equity* consists of chapters emphasizing expressions of social equity values, contextual philosophies and abstractions and procedures absent specific detail about patterns of fairness in specific policy fields such as education or housing.

The second half of the book moves the subject from abstraction toward applications. Starting with a detailed treatment of those aspects of social equity that are intergenerational, chapter 6 is an in-depth consideration of the specifics of, for example, capital budgeting and long-range borrowing as applied intergenerational fairness. The analysis in chapter 6 ranges all the way from the intergenerational transfer of the values of fairness, justice, and equity, both in the general population and among public officials, to the legacy public structure and infrastructure passed from one generation to the next. The chapter is about the intersections of time, political culture, and the social equity perspective in public administration.

Chapter 7 goes directly to the details of policy specificity. At the center of democratic public policy is the law, regulation pursuant to the law, and the public administration practices of policy implementation. Each policy arena is unique, and issues of social equity in each are also unique. It is at the policy level that the most important research is being done on social equity. Consider, as illustrative of the point, Steven Maynard-Moody and Michael Musheno's *Cops, Teachers, Counselors: Stories from the Front Lines of Public Service*, a richly empirical treatment of the exercise of discretion by street-level bureaucrats attempting to be fair in the context of scarce resources. Each policy field is the subject of similar empirical research. Because most of this research is by scholars in other fields, one of the most pressing research challenges for social equity specialists in public administration is the distillation and synthesis of this research and its application to public administration.

Modern public administration is in part built on the logic of individual merit. Merit and specialized competence and standards of individual appointment and advancement, standards are designed to ensure the effective administration of government and to eliminate or at least lessen the influence of partisan politics in administration. Over the past century, it is generally understood that through the logic of merit, based on education, tests, and experience, modern public administration has reduced government corruption and increased government effectiveness. Merit, however, is often little more than a reflection of social and economic advantage and a means by which advantage may be perpetuated. How, therefore, can fairness and equity find a place in a world of merit-based public administration. Chapter 8 is treatment of this conundrum in the field of education and in the public schools. Public education is an excellent topic to consider if one wishes to explore the tensions between educational quality on one hand and educational equality on the other. It is, after all, in the field of education that the effectiveness of the schools has been under relentless attack on the basis of "poor quality," quality being the equivalent of merit. In the context of the "No Child Left Behind" Act of 2001 (www.ed.gov/policy/elsec/leg/esea02/) the "failure" of schools, based on testing, is directly attributed to poor teachers. As the implementation of NCLB has played out in recent years, however, it has become increasingly evident that poor schooling is uniquely associated with poverty, poor housing, unemployment, and other social disadvantages.

The tension between merit or quality on one hand and fairness or equity on the other, applied in some depth in the field of public education in chapter 8, is taken up in a different way in chapter 9. Written as an imaginary conversation between Philip J. Rutledge, who had just died, and a group of public administration social equity scholars, this chapter discusses the opinions and perspectives of the leading social equity theorists and scholars of the early twenty-first century. The works of Seymour Martin Lipset and Walter Ben Michael are given particular emphasis.

Chapter 10, the conclusion, is a loose attempt at synthesis and the "light phenomenology" referred to early in this introduction. To return there briefly, both the concepts and practices of social equity have, over the past forty years, found a permanent place in the public administration canon. This book claims that social equity is now a better understanding of a set of values and preferences, a clearer array of policies and procedures, and a steadily growing body of research based on analysis. While not as well developed theoretically or the subject of as much research and analysis as efficiency and economy, social equity is a strengthening third pillar of public administration.

Social Equity and Public Administration

1

Social Equity and the New Public Administration

Written in 1969, the following is the original essay on social equity in public administration (Marini 1971). Reprinted in readers and anthologies dozens of times, it is covered in most public administration texts and is widely referenced both in English and other languages. Although the word "equity" appears in the original Woodrow Wilson ([1887] 1941) essay and in other public administration classics, this essay is the first relatively full elaboration of the concept of social equity and its application to public administration. And, it is the first to claim that social equity should form part of the normative base of public administration.

As mentioned in the Introduction, this essay was written at the height of the social turbulence of the late 1960s and early 1970s. It traces directly to the original Minnowbrook Conference, also described in the Introduction. Most of the essays in *Toward a New Public Administration: The Minnowbrook Perspective* (Marini 1971), the book that covers the original Minnowbrook Conference, were written in advance of the gathering. The essay appearing here is one of three essays in *Toward a New Public Administration* by the conference organizers (H. George Frederickson, W. Henry Lambright, and Frank Marini) that were written after the conference. With the considerable advantage of having read the other Minnowbrook essays, these authors were invited to summarize and synthesize the earlier writings or to identify an important new theme and develop it. In writing the essay that follows, I obviously chose the second alternative.

It is particularly important to account for the connections between the so-called new public administration and the phrase "social equity." New public administration was in part a reflection of the spirit of the times, an

Adapted and updated from *Toward a New Public Administration: The Minnowbrook Perspective*, ed. Frank Marini (Scranton: Chandler, 1971). Used by permission of Chandler Sharp Publishers.

expression of disappointment in the state of the field and a rallying cry for a new, changed, and presumably better public administration. The use of the phrase "new public administration" was to some extent understood to provoke and to draw attention. New public administration also had the advantage of being broad, so broad in fact, that most any perspective or approach to public administration could identify with it. Several of the perspectives or approaches that identified with the new public administration are still quite evident in the field, including social equity. And the tradition of Minnowbrook, a generational critique of the field by younger scholars, is very much alive, as the Minnowbrook III meeting held in September of 2008 serves to illustrate. But, as an identifiable and easily describable movement, the new public administration did not last, in large part because it was too broad and too provocative. By the mid-1980s, the phrase "new public administration" was seldom heard outside of the textbooks.

The importance of the social equity perspective in public administration has waxed and waned over the past forty years, but it has survived and taken its place as part of both the normative base of the field and as the subject of considerable empirical research.

As the reader will note, in the original essay on social equity in public administration, it was assumed that social equity was part of the new public administration. It is interesting that the title of the original essay on social equity was "Toward a New Public Administration," and not social equity, although that was clearly the subject.

Because the essay that follows was written at another time and under very different circumstances, some of the examples and references require a bit of interpretation.

There are several references to "program-planning-budgeting systems" or PPBs, an early mix of those aspects of strategic planning that have to do with goal and mission identification with performance measurement and performance budgeting. At the time, PPB was a kind of administrative and political movement rather like one sees today in the strategic planning movement, the logic upon which are based both on the Government Performance and Results Act of 1993 and the modern performance measurement and performance budgeting "movement." PPB lost its momentum and support when it was determined that a measure of progress in the Vietnam War was comparing Vietnamese and American body counts.

In the following essay, there are references to forms of "confrontational" administration based on social equity. A modern and particularly impressive presentation of some of the same logic in a somewhat different language is found in Rosemary O'Leary's recent book *The Ethics of Dissent: Managing Guerrilla Government* (Washington, DC: CQ Press, 2006). It appears that the logic of some forms of social equity–based administrative confrontation is alive and well.

There are several references to project management in government. In contemporary times these "projects" would in fact be contracts and those engaged in these projects would not be civil servants but contractors.

The essay calls for some rather idealistic forms of client or citizen involvement in administrative policymaking and implementation. This was well before the days of the modern civic engagement or civil society movement. Although not at all sophisticated, the arguments about client involvement are rather like the modern "bowling alone" thesis and the rather strong civic capital movement.

There is a section in the essay on the so-called socioemotional approach to public administration based on role theory, group theory, organizational development training, and other aspects of more democratic forms of organization and management. On reflection it seemed at the time that genuine new public administration called not only for better policies, procedures, and processes, it called for better people. Making people, including administrators, better could be done, so it seemed, by emotional forms of training. While there are still some adherents to the so-called organizational development perspective, it is no longer connected to the social equity perspective.

Finally, the essay calls for a stronger emphasis on policy studies in the graduate study of public administration. It is interesting that not long after the publication of this essay, there began to be separate graduate programs in public policy studies. But, rather than build policy studies into the study of public administration, these programs discontinued their public administration programs and replaced them wholesale with policy analysis (later policy studies) programs. Not long after that the Ford Foundation funded new public policy analysis graduate programs at several prestigious universities (such as Harvard and Berkeley). In many ways, these steps were more radical than those anticipated by those associated with the early development of social equity. Today social equity is explicitly part of the theory and the practice of public administration. And, issues of fairness and justice are prominent in policy analysis and policy studies. In many ways they are the same thing.

⊓

In full recognition of the risks, this is an essay on new public administration. Its first purpose is to present my interpretation and synthesis of new public administration as it emerged at the Minnowbrook Conference on new public administration. This synthesis is based on an introduction of the concept of said equity and the initial application of social equity to public administration. Its second purpose is to describe how this interpretation and synthesis of new public administration relates to the wider world of administrative thought and practice. And its third purpose is to interpret what new public administration means for organization theory and vice versa.

To affix the label "new" to anything is risky business. The risk is doubled when newness is attributed to ideas, thoughts, concepts, paradigms, theories. Those who claim new thinking tend to regard previous thought as old or jejune or both. In response, the authors of previous thought are defensive and inclined to suggest that, "aside from having packaged earlier thinking in a new vocabulary there is little that is really new in so-called new thinking." Accept, therefore, this caveat: Parts of new public administration would be recognized by Plato, Hobbes, Machiavelli, Hamilton, and Jefferson as well as many modern behavioral theorists. The newness is in the way the fabric is woven, not necessarily in the threads that are used, and in arguments as to the proper use of the fabric—however threadbare.

The threads of the public administration fabric are well known. Herbert Kaufman describes them simply as the pursuit of these basic values: representativeness, politically neutral competence, and executive leadership (Kaufman 1969). In different times, one or the other of these values receives the greatest emphasis. Representativeness was preeminent in the Jacksonian era. The eventual reaction was the reform movement emphasizing neutral competence and executive leadership. Now we are witnessing a revolt against these values accompanied by a search for new modes of representativeness.

Others have argued that changes in public administration resemble a zero-sum game between administrative efficiency and political responsiveness. Any increase in efficiency results a priori in a decrease in responsiveness. We are simply entering a period during which political responsiveness is to be purchased at a cost in administrative efficiency.

Both the dichotomous and trichotomous value models of public administration just described are correct as gross generalizations. But they suffer the weakness of gross generalizations: They fail to account for the wide, often rich, and sometimes subtle variation that rests within. Moreover, the generalization does not explain those parts of public administration that are beyond its sweep. Describing what new public administration means for organization theory is a process by which these generalizations can be given substance. But first it is necessary to briefly sketch what this student means by new public administration.

What Is New Public Administration?

Educators have as their basic objective, and most convenient rationale, expanding and transmitting knowledge. The police are enforcing the law. Public-health agencies lengthen life by fighting disease. Then there are firemen, sanitation men, welfare workers, diplomats, the military, and so forth. All are employed by public agencies and each specialization or profession has its own substantive set of objectives and therefore its rationale.

What, then, is public administration (Mosher 1967, Honey 1967)? What are its objectives and its rationale?

The classic answer has always been the efficient, economical, and coordinated management of the services listed above. The focus has been on top-level management (city management as an example) or the basic auxiliary staff services (budgeting, organization and management, systems analysis, planning, personnel, purchasing). The rationale for public administration is almost always better (more efficient or economical) management. New public administration adds social equity to the classic objectives and rationale. Conventional or classic public administration seeks to answer either of these questions: (1) How can we offer more or better services with available resources (efficiency)? or (2) How can we maintain our level of services while spending less money (economy)? New public administration adds this question: Does this service enhance social equity?

The phrase social equity is used here to summarize the following set of value premises. Pluralistic democratic government systematically discriminates in favor of established stable bureaucracies and their specialized minority clientele (the Department of Agriculture and large farmers as an example) and against those minorities (farm laborers, both migrant and permanent, as an example) who lack political and economic resources. The continuation of widespread unemployment, poverty, disease, ignorance, and hopelessness in an era of unprecedented economic growth is the result. This condition is morally reprehensible and if left unchanged constitutes a fundamental, if long-range, threat to the viability of this or any political system. Continued deprivation amid plenty breeds widespread militancy. Militancy is followed by repression, which is followed by greater militancy, and so forth. A public administration which fails to work for changes that try to redress the deprivation of minorities will likely be eventually used to repress those minorities.

For a variety of reasons—probably the most important being committee legislatures, seniority legislatures, entrenched bureaucracies, nondemocratized political-party procedures, inequitable revenue-raising capacity in the lesser governments of the federal system—the procedures of representative democracy presently operate in a way that either fails or only very gradually attempts to reverse systematic discrimination against disadvantaged minorities. Social equity, then, includes activities designed to enhance the political power and economic well being of these minorities.

A fundamental commitment to social equity means that new public administration attempts to come to grips with Dwight Waldo's contention that the field has never satisfactorily accommodated the theoretical implications of involvement in "politics" and policy making (Waldo 1968). The policy-administration dichotomy lacks an empirical warrant, for it is abundantly clear that administrators both execute and make policy. The policy-administration continuum is more accurate empirically but simply begs the theoretical question. New public administration attempts to answer it in this way: Administrators are not neutral. They should be committed to both good management and social equity as values, things to be achieved, or rationales.

A fundamental commitment to social equity means that new public administration is anxiously engaged in change. Simply put, new public administration seeks to change those policies and structures that systematically inhibit social equity. This is not seeking change for change's sake nor is it advocating alterations in the relative roles of administrators, executives, legislators, or the courts in our basic constitutional forms. Educators, agriculturists, police, and the like can work for changes which enhance their objectives and resist those that threaten those objectives, all within the framework of our governmental system. New public administration works in the same way to seek the changes which would enhance its objectives—good management, efficiency, economy, and social equity.

A commitment to social equity not only involves the pursuit of change but attempts to find organizational and political forms which exhibit a capacity for continued flexibility or routinized change. Traditional bureaucracy has a demonstrated capacity for stability, indeed, ultrastability (Downs 1967). New public administration, in its search for changeable structures, tends therefore to experiment with or advocate modified bureaucratic-organizational forms. Decentralization, devolution, projects, contracts, sensitivity training, organization development, responsibility expansion, confrontation, and client involvement are all essentially counterbureaucratic notions that characterize new public administration. These concepts are designed to enhance both bureaucratic and policy change and thus to increase possibilities for social equity. Indeed, an important faculty member in one of the best-known and larger master of public administration programs in the country described that degree program as "designed to produce change agents or specialists in organizational development."

Other organizational notions such as programming-planning-budgeting systems, executive inventories, and social indicators can be seen as enhancing change in the direction of social equity. They are almost always presented in terms of good management (witness McNamara and PPB) as a basic strategy, because it is unwise to frontally advocate change (Schultze 1969). In point of fact, however, PPB can be used as a basic device for change (in McNamara's case to attempt to wrest control from the uniformed services, but in the name of efficiency and economy). The executive inventory can be used to alter the character of the top levels of a particular bureaucracy, thereby enhancing change possibilities. Social indicators are designed to show variation in socioeconomic circumstances in the hope that attempts will be made to improve the conditions of those who are shown to be disadvantaged (Bauer 1967). All three of these notions have only a surface neutrality or good management character. Under the surface they are devices by which administrators and executives try to bring about change. It is no wonder they are so widely favored in public administration circles. And it should not be surprising that economists and political scientists in the "pluralist" camp regard devices such as PPB as fundamentally threatening to their conception of democratic government (Wildavsky 1964; Lindblom 1965). Although they are more subtle in terms of change, PPB, executive inventories, and social indicators are of the same genre as more frontal change techniques such as sensitivity training, projects, contracts, decentralization, and the like. All enhance change, and change is basic to new public administration.

New public administration's commitment to social equity implies a strong administrative or executive government—what Hamilton called "energy in the executive." The policy-making powers of the administrative parts of government are increasingly recognized. In addition, a fundamentally new form of political access and representativeness is now occurring in the administration of government and it may be that this access and representativeness is as critical to major policy decisions as is legislative access or representativeness. New public administration seeks not only to carry out legislative mandates as efficiently and economically as possible, but to both influence and execute policies which more generally improve the quality of life for all. Forthright policy advocacy on the part of the public servant is essential if administrative agencies are basic policy battlefields. New public administrationists are likely to be forthright advocates for social equity and will doubtless seek a supporting clientele.

Classic public administration emphasizes developing and strengthening institutions which have been designed to deal with social problems. The public administration focus, however, has tended to drift from the problem to the institution. New public administration attempts to refocus on the problem and to consider alternative possible institutional approaches to confronting problems. The intractable character of many public problems such as urban poverty, widespread narcotics use, high crime rates, and the like lead public administrators to seriously question the investment of ever more money and manpower in institutions which seem only to worsen the problems. They seek, therefore, either to modify these institutions or develop new and more easily changed ones designed to achieve more proximate solutions. New public administration is concerned less with the Defense Department than with defense, less with civil-service commissions than with the manpower needs of administrative agencies on the one hand and the employment needs of the society on the other, less with building institutions and more with designing alternate means of solving public problems. These alternatives will no doubt have some recognizable organizational characteristics and they will need to be built and maintained but will seek to avoid becoming entrenched, nonresponsive bureaucracies that become greater public problems than the social situations they were originally designed to improve.

The movement from an emphasis on institution building and maintenance to an emphasis on social anomalies has an important analogue in the study of public administration. The last generation of students of public administration generally accept both Simon's logical positivism and his call for an empirically based organization theory. They focus on generic concepts such as decision, role, and group theory to develop a generalizable body of organization theory. The search is for commonalities of behavior in all organizational settings (March and Simon 1963). The organization and the people within it are the empirical referent. The product is usually description, not prescription, and if it is prescription it prescribes how to better manage the organization internally. The subject matter is first organization and second the type of organization—private, public, voluntary (Etzioni 1961). The two main bodies of theory emerging from this generation of work are decision theory and human-relation theory. Both are regarded as behavioral and positivist. Both are at least as heavily influenced by sociology, social psychology, and economics as they are by political science.

New public administration advocates what could be best described as "second-generation behavioralism." Unlike his progenitor, the second-generation behavioralist emphasizes the public part of public administration. He accepts the importance of understanding as scientifically as possible how and why organizations behave as they do but he tends to be rather more interested in the impact of that organization on its clientele and vice versa. He is not antipositivist nor antiscientific although he is probably less than sanguine about the applicability of the natural-science model to social phenomena. He is not likely to use his behavioralism as a rationale for simply trying to describe how public organizations behave.[1] Nor is he inclined to use his behavioralism as a facade for so-called neutrality, being more than a little skeptical of the objectivity of those who claim to be doing science. He attempts to use his scientific skills to aid his analysis, experimentation, and evaluation of alternative policies and administrative modes. In sum, then, the second-generation behavioralist is less "generic" and more "public" than his forebear, less "descriptive" and more "prescriptive," less "institution oriented" and more "client-impact oriented," less "neutral" and more "normative," and, it is hoped, no less scientific.

This has been a brief and admittedly surface description of new public administration from the perspective of one analyst. If the description is even partially accurate it is patently clear that there are fundamental changes occurring in public administration which have salient implications for both its study and practice as well as for the general conduct of government. The final purpose of this chapter is a consideration of the likely impact of new public administration on organization theory particularly and the study of administration generally. (The term "theory" is used here in its loose sense, as abstract thought.)

Organization Theory and New Public Administration

Understanding any phenomenon requires separating that phenomenon into parts and examining each part in detail. In understanding government this separation can reflect institutions such as the traditional "fields" in political science—public administration, legislative behavior, public law, and so forth. Or this separation can be primarily conceptual or theoretical such as systems theory, decision theory, role theory, group theory all of which cut across institutions.

Public administration has never had either an agreed upon or a satisfactory set of subfields. The "budgeting," "personnel administration," "organization and management" categories are too limiting, too "inside-organization" oriented, and too theoretically vacant. The middle-range theories—decisions, roles, groups, and the like—are stronger theoretically and have yielded more empirically, but still tend to focus almost exclusively on the internal dynamics of public organizations. The new public administration calls for a different way of subdividing the phenomenon so as to better understand it. This analyst suggests that there are four basic processes at work in public organizations and further suggests that these processes are suitable for both understanding and improving public administration. The four suggested processes are: the distributive process; the integrative process; the boundary-exchange process; and the socioemotional process.

The Distributive Process

New public administration is vitally concerned with patterns of distribution. This concern has to do first with the external distribution of goods and services to particular categories of persons, in terms of the benefits that result from the operation of publicly administered programs.

Cost-utility, or cost-benefit, analysis is the chief technique for attempting to understand the results of the distributive process. This form of analysis presumes to measure the utility to individuals of particular public programs. Because it attempts to project the likely costs and benefits of alternative programs it is a very central part of new public administration. It is central primarily because it provides a scientific or quasi-scientific means for attempting to "get at" the question of equity. It also provides a convenient or classic public administration rationale for redistribution.

Because of the emergence of "program-planning-budgeting systems" we are beginning to see, in the policy advocacy of the various bureaus and departments of government, their attempts to demonstrate their impact on society in terms of utility. Wildavsky and Lindblom have argued that rational or cost-utility analysis is difficult if not impossible to do. Further, they contend, rational decision making fundamentally alters or changes our political system by dealing with basic political questions within the arena of the administrator. To date they are essentially correct, empirically. Normatively they are apologists for pluralism. Cost-benefit analysis can be an effective means by which inequities can be demonstrated. It is a tool by which legislatures and entrenched bureaucracies can be caused to defend publicly their distributive decisions. The inference is that a public informed of glaring inequities will demand change.

Like the executive budget, rational or cost-benefit decision systems (PPB) enhance the power of executives and administrators and are, again, a part of new public administration. Because PPB is being widely adopted in cities and states, as well as in the national government, it seems clear that new public administration will be highly visible simply by a look at the distributive processes of government over the next decade or two. The extent to which PPB will result in a redistribution which enhances social equity remains to be seen.

Benefit or utility analysis in its less prescriptive and more descriptive form, known in political science as "policy-outcomes analysis," attempts to determine the basic factors that influence or determine policy variation (Fenton and Chamberlayne 1969). For example, "outcomes analysts" sketch the relationship between variations in public spending (quantity) and the quality of nonspending policy outcomes. The policy-outcomes analyst attempts to determine the relationship between the levels of spending in education and the IQs, employability, college admissibility, and the like of the products of the educational process. This analysis is essentially after the fact, and indeed is commonly based on relatively out-of-date census data. It is, therefore, useful to new public administration, but only as a foundation or background.

A newer form of distributive analysis is emerging. This approach focuses on equity in the distribution of government services within a jurisdiction and asks questions such as: Does a school board distribute its funds equitably to schools and to the school children in its jurisdiction, and if not is inequity in the direction of the advantaged or disadvantaged? Are sanitation services distributed equitably to all neighborhoods in the city, and if not in what direction does inequity move and how is it justified? Is state and federal aid distributed equitably, and if not how are inequities justified?[2]

Patterns of internal-organization distribution are a traditional part of organization theory. The internal competition for money, manpower, status, space, and priorities is a staple in organization theory as any reading of the Administrative Science Quarterly indicates. We learn from this literature the extent to which many of the functions of government are in essence controlled by particular bodies of professionals—educators, physicians, attorneys, social workers, and the like. We learn how agencies age and become rigid and devote much of their energies to competing for survival. We learn the extent to which distribution becomes what Wildavsky calls a triangulation between bureaus, legislatures (particularly legislative committees), and elected executives and their auxiliary staffs (Wildavsky 1964). Finally, we have whole volumes of aggregated and disaggregated hypotheses which account for or attempt to explain the decision patterns involved in the internal distributive process (March and Simon 1963; Downs 1967; Price 1968).

In new public administration the internal distributive process is likely to involve somewhat less readiness to make incremental compromises or "bargain" and somewhat more "administrative confrontation." If new public administrators are located in the staff agencies of the executive, which is highly likely, they will doubtless be considerably more tenacious than their predecessors. The spokesman for an established agency might have learned to pad his budget, to overstaff, to control public access to records, and to expand his space in preparation for the compromises he has learned to expect. He might now encounter a zealot armed with data which describe in detail padding, overstaffing, and suppressed records. Therefore an organization theory based primarily on the traditional administrative bargaining process is likely to be woefully inadequate. There is a need to develop a theory that accounts for the presence of public administrators considerably less willing to bargain and more willing to take political and administrative risks.

It is difficult to predict the possible consequences of having generalist public administrators who are prepared to rationalize their positions and decisions on the basis of social equity. Administrative theory explains relatively well the results of the use of efficiency, economy, or good management as rationale. We know, for instance, that these arguments are especially persuasive in years in which legislatures and elected executives do not wish to raise taxes.

But we also know that virtually anything can be justified under the rubric "good management." When public administrators leave the safe harbor of this rhetoric, what might occur? The best guess is a more open conflict on basic issues of goals or purposes. Some administrators will triumph, but the majority will not; for the system tends to work against those seeking change and willing to take risks for it. The result is likely to be a highly mobile and relatively unstable middle-level civil service. Still, actual withdrawal or removal from the system after a major setback is likely to be preferred by new public administrators to the psychic withdrawal which is now common among administrators.

One can imagine, for instance, a city personnel director prepared to confront the chief of police and the police bureaucracy on the question of eligibility standards for new patrolmen. He might argue, backed with considerable data, that patrolman height and weight regulations are unrealistic and systematically discriminate against deprived minorities. He might also argue that misdemeanor convictions by minors should not prohibit adults from becoming patrolmen. If this were an open conflict, it would likely array deprived minorities against the majority of the city council, possibly against the mayor, and certainly against the chief and his men (and no doubt the unions). While the new public administrator might be perfectly willing to take the risks involved in such a confrontation, present theory does not accommodate well what this means for the political system generally.

The Integrative Process

Authority hierarchies are the primary means by which the work of persons in publicly administrated organizations is coordinated. The formal hierarchy is the most obvious and easiest-to-identify part of the permanent and on-going organization. Administrators are seen as persons taking roles in the hierarchy and performing tasks that are integrated through the hierarchies to constitute a cohesive goal-seeking whole. The public administrator has customarily been regarded as the one who builds and maintains the organization through the hierarchy. He or she attempts to understand formal-informal relationships, status, politics, and power in authority hierarchies. The hierarchy is at once an ideal design and a hospitable environment for the person who wishes to manage, control, or direct the work of large numbers of people. The counterproductive characteristics of hierarchies are well known (V.A. Thomson 1961; Presthus 1962). New public administration is probably best understood as advocating modified hierarchic systems. Several means both in theory and practice are utilized to modify traditional hierarchies. The first and perhaps the best known is the project or matrix technique (Cleland and King 1968, 1969; Steiner and

Ryan 1968; Baumgartner 1963). The project is, by definition, temporary. The project manager and his or her staff are a team that attempts to utilize the services of regularly established hierarchies in an ongoing organization. For the duration of the project, the manager must get his or her technical services from the technical hierarchy of the organization, his or her personnel services from the personnel agency, his or her budgeting services from the budget department, and so forth. Obviously the project technique would not be effective were it not for considerable top-level support for the project. When there are conflicts between the needs of the project and the survival needs of established hierarchies, top management must consistently decide in favor of the projects. The chief advantage of projects is of course their collapsible nature. While bureaucracies seldom disestablish or self-destruct, projects do. The project concept is especially useful when associated with "one time" hardware or research and development, or capital improvement efforts. The concept is highly sophisticated in engineering circles and theoretically could be applied to a large number of less technical and more social problems. The project technique is also useful as a device by which government contracts with industry can be monitored and coordinated.

Other procedures for modifying hierarchies are well known and include the group-decision-making model, the link-pin function, and the so-called dialectical organization (Likert 1961; White 1969). And, of course, true decentralization is a fundamental modification hierarchy (Kaufman 1969).

Exploration and experimentation with these various techniques is a basic part of new public administration. The search for less structured, less formal, and less authoritative integrative techniques in publicly administered organizations is only beginning. The preference for these types of organizational modes implies first a relatively high tolerance for variation. This includes variations in administrative performance and variations in procedures and applications based upon differences in clients or client groups. It also implies great tolerance for the possibilities of inefficiency and diseconomy. In a very general sense this preference constitutes a willingness to trade increases in involvement and commitment to the organization for possible decreases in efficiency and economy, particularly in the short run. In the long run, less formal and less authoritative integrative techniques may prove to be more efficient and economical.

There are two serious problems with the advocacy by new public administration of less formal integrative processes. First, there may be a lack of public administration specialists who are essentially program builders. The new public administration person who is trained as a change agent and an advocate of informal, decentralized, integrative processes may not be capable of building and maintaining large, permanent organizations. This problem may not be serious, however, because administrators in the several professions (education, law enforcement, welfare, and the like) are often capable organization builders, or at least protectors, so a public administration specialist can concentrate on the change or modification of hierarchies built by others.

The second problem is the inherent conflict between higher- and lower-level administrators in less formal, integrative systems. While describing the distributive process in public administration it was quite clear that top-level public administrators were to be strong and assertive. In this description of the integrative process there is a marked preference for large degrees of autonomy at the base of the organization. The only way to theoretically accommodate this contradiction is through an organizational design in which top-level public administrators are regarded as policy advocates and general-policy reviewers. If they have a rather high tolerance for the variations in policy application then it can be presumed that intermediate and lower levels in the organization can apply wide interpretive license in program application. This accommodation is a feeble one, to be sure, but higher-lower-level administrative relations are a continuing problem in public administration, and the resolution of these problems in the past has tended to be in the direction of the interests of upper levels of the hierarchy in combination with subdivisions of the legislative body and potent interest groups. New public administration searches for a means by which lower levels of the organization and less potent minorities can be favored.

The Boundary-Exchange Process

The boundary-exchange process describes the general relationship between the publicly administered organization and its reference groups and clients. These include legislatures, elected executives, auxiliary staff organizations, clients (both organized and individual), and organized interest groups. The boundary-exchange process also accounts for the relationship between levels of government in a federal system. Because publicly administered organizations find themselves in a competitive political, social, and economic environment, they tend to seek support. This is done by first finding a clientele which can play a strong advocacy role with the legislature, then by developing a symbiotic relationship between the agency and key committees or members of the legislature, followed by building and maintaining as permanent an organization as is possible.

The distributive and integrative processes that have just been described call for vastly altered concepts of how to conduct boundary exchange in new public administration (J.D. Thompson 1967). Future organization theory will have to accommodate the following pattern of boundary exchange. First, a considerably higher client involvement is necessary on the part of those minorities who have not heretofore been involved. (It is unfair to assume that minorities are not already involved as clients; farmers, bankers, and heavy industries are minorities and they are highly involved clients. In this sense all public organizations are "client" oriented.) This change probably spells a different kind of involvement. A version of this kind of involvement is now being seen in some of our cities as a result of militancy and community-action programs, and on the campuses of some universities. A preferred form of deprived-minority-client involvement would be routinized patterns of communication with decentralized organizations capable of making distributive decisions that support the interests of deprived minorities, even if these decisions are difficult to justify in terms of either efficiency or economy.

In a very general way, this kind of decision making occurs in time of war with respect to military decision making. It also characterizes decision patterns in the program of the National Aeronautics and Space Administration. These two examples characterize crash programs designed to solve problems that are viewed as immediate and pressing. They involve a kind of backward budgeting in which large blocks of funds are made available for the project and wide latitude in expenditures is tolerated. The detailed accounting occurs after the spending, not before, hence backward budgeting. Under these conditions what to do and what materials are needed are decided at low levels of the organization. These decisions are made on the presumption that they will be supported and the necessary resources will be made available and accounted for by upper levels of the organization. This same logic could clearly be applied to the ghetto. A temporary project could be established in which the project manager and his staff work with the permanently established bureaucracies in a city in a crash program designed to solve the employment, housing, health, education, and transportation needs of the residents of that ghetto. The decisions and procedures of one project would likely vary widely from those of another, based on the differences in the circumstances of the clientele involved and the political-administrative environments encountered. The central project director would tolerate the variations both in decisions and patterns of expenditures in the same way that the Department of Defense and NASA cover their expenditures in times of crisis.

The danger will be in the tendency of decentralized projects to be taken over by local pluralist elites. The U.S. Selective Service is an example of this kind of takeover. High levels of disadvantaged-minority-client involvement are necessary to offset this tendency. Still, it will be difficult to prevent the new controlling minorities from systematic discrimination against the old controlling minorities.

From this description of a boundary-exchange relationship, it is probably safe to predict that administrative agencies, particularly those that are decentralized, will increasingly become the primary means by which particular minorities find their basic form of political representation. This situation exists now in the case of the highly advantaged minorities and may very well become the case with the disadvantaged.

The means by which high client involvement is to be secured is problematic. The maximum-feasible-participation notion, although given a very bad press, was probably more successful than most analysts are prepared to admit. Maximum feasible participation certainly did not enhance the efficiency or economy of the activities of the Office of Equal Opportunities, but, and perhaps most important, it gave the residents of the ghetto at least the impression that they had the capacity to influence publicly made decisions that affected their well being. High client involvement probably means, first, the employment of the disadvantaged where feasible; second, the use of client review boards or review agencies; and third, decentralized legislatures such as the kind sought by the Brownhill School District in the New York City Board of Education decentralization controversy.

The development of this pattern of boundary exchange spells the probable development of new forms of intergovernmental relations, particularly fiscal relations. Federal grants-in-aid to states and cities, and state grants-in-aid to cities will no doubt be expanded, and probably better equalized (Wright 1968). In addition, some form of tax sharing is probably called for. The fundamental weakness of the local governments' revenue capacity must be alleviated.

The use of the distributive and integrative processes described above probably also means the development of new means by which administrators relate to their legislatures. The elected official will probably always hold continuance in office as his or her number-one objective. This means that a public administration using less formal integrative processes must find means by which it can enhance the reelection probabilities of supporting incumbents. Established centralized bureaucracies do this in a variety of ways, the best known being building and maintaining of roads or other capital facilities in the legislator's district, establishing high-employment facilities, such as federal office buildings, county courthouses, police precincts, and the like, and distributing public-relations materials favorable to the incumbent legislator. The decentralized organization seems especially suited for the provision of this kind of service for legislators. As a consequence it is entirely possible to imagine legislators becoming strong spokesmen for less hierarchic and less authoritative bureaucracies.

The Socioemotional Process

The public administration described herein will require both individual and group characteristics that differ from those presently seen. The widespread use of sensitivity training, T techniques, or "organizational development" is compatible with new public administration. These techniques include lowering an individual's reliance on hierarchy, enabling him to tolerate conflict and emotions, and indeed under certain circumstances to welcome them, and to prepare him to take greater risks. From the preceding discussion it is clear that sensitizing techniques are parallel to the distributive, integrative, and boundary-exchange processes just described.

Socioemotional training techniques are fundamental devices for administrative change. These techniques have thus far been used primarily to strengthen or redirect on-going and established bureaucracies. In the future it is expected that the same techniques will be utilized to aid in the development of decentralized and possibly project-oriented organizational modes.

A recent assessment of the U.S. Department of State by Chris Argyris is highly illustrative of the possible impact of new public administration on organizational socioemotional processes (Argyris 1966). Argyris concluded that "State" is a social system characterized by individual withdrawal from interpersonal difficulties and conflict; minimum interpersonal openness, leveling, and trust; a withdrawal from aggressiveness and fighting; the view that being emotional is being ineffective or irrational; leaders' domination of subordinates; an unawareness of leaders' personal impact on others; and very high levels of conformity coupled with low levels of risk taking or responsibility taking. To correct these organizational "pathologies" Argyris recommended that:

1. A long-range change program should be defined with the target being to change the living system of the State Department.
2. The first stage of the change program should focus on the behavior and leadership style of the most senior participants within the Department of State.
3. Simultaneously with the involvement of the top, similar change activities should be initiated in any subpart which shows signs of being ready for change.
4. The processes of organizational change and development that are created should require the same behavior and attitudes as those we wish to inculcate into the system (take more initiative, enlarge responsibilities, take risks).

5. As the organizational development activities produce a higher level of leadership skills and begin to reduce the system's defenses in the area of interpersonal relations, the participants should be helped to begin to reexamine some of the formal policies and activities of the State Department that presently may act as inhibitors to organizational effectiveness (employee evaluations and ratings, promotion process, inspections). The reexamination should be conducted under the direction of line executives with the help of inside or outside consultants.

6. The similarities and interdependencies between administration and substance need to be made more explicit and more widely accepted.

7. The State Department's internal capacity in the new areas of behavioral-science-based knowledge should be increased immediately.

8. Long-range research programs should be developed, exploring the possible value of the behavioral disciplines to the conduct of diplomacy.

The characteristics of the State Department are, sad to say, common in publicly administered organizations. While Argyris's recommendations are particular to "State," they are relevant to all highly authoritative hierarchy-based organizations.

While new public administration is committed to wider social equity, the foregoing should make it clear that a more nearly equitable internal organization is also an objective.

Conclusions

The search for social equity provides public administration with a real normative base. Like many value premises, social equity has the ring of flag, country, mother, and apple pie. But surely the pursuit of social equity in public administration is no more a holy grail than the objectives of educators, medical doctors, and so forth. Still, it appears that new public administration is an alignment with good, or possibly God.

What are the likely results for a practicing public administration working from such a normative base? First, classic public administration on the basis of its expressed objectives commonly had the support of businessmen and the articulate and educated upper and upper-middle classes. The phenomenal success of the municipal-reform movement is testament to this. If new public administration attempts to justify or rationalize its stance on the basis of social equity, it might have to augment support from its traditional sources with support from the disadvantaged minorities. It might be possible for new public administration to continue to receive support from the educated and articulate if we assume that this social class is becoming increasingly committed to those public programs that are equity enhancing and less committed to those that are not. Nevertheless, it appears that new public administration should be prepared to take the risks involved in such a trade, if it is necessary to do so.

Second, new public administration, in its quest for social equity, might encounter the kinds of opposition that the Supreme Court has experienced in the last decade. That is to say, substantial opposition from elected officials for its fundamental involvement in shaping social policy. The Court, because of its independence, is less vulnerable than administration. We might expect, therefore, greater legislative controls over administrative agencies and particularly the distributive patterns of such agencies.

Third, new public administration might well foster a political system in which elected officials speak basically for the majority and for interest groups while courts and the administrators are spokesmen for disadvantaged minorities. As administrators work in behalf of the equitable distribution of public and private goods, courts are increasingly interpreting the Constitution in the same direction. Legislative hostility to this activity might be directed at administration simply because it is most vulnerable.

What of new public administration and academia? First let us consider the theory, then the academy. Organization theory will be influenced by new public administration in a variety of ways. The uniqueness of public organization will be stressed. Internal administrative behavior, the forte of the generic administration school and the foundation of much of what is now known as organization theory, will be a part of scholarly public administration, but will be less central. Its center position in public administration will be taken by a strong emphasis on the distributive and boundary-exchange processes described above.

Quantitatively inclined public-organization theorists are likely to drift toward or at least read widely in welfare economics. Indeed it is possible to imagine these theorists executing a model or paradigm of social equity fully as robust as the economist's market model. With social equity elevated to the supreme objective, in much the way profit is treated in economics, model building is relatively simple. We might, for example, develop theories of equity maximization, long- and short-range equity, equity elasticity, and so on. The theory and research being reported in the journal *Public Choice* provides a glimpse of this probable development. This work is presently being done primarily by economists who are, in the main, attempting to develop variations on the market model or notions of individual-utility maximization. Public organization theorists with social-equity commitments could contribute greatly by the creation of models less fixed on market environments or individual-utility maximization and more on the equitable distribution of and access to both public and private goods by different groups or categories of people. If a full-blown equity model were developed it might be possible to assess rather precisely the likely outcomes of alternative policies in terms of whether the alternative does or does not enhance equity. Schemes for guaranteed annual income, negative income tax, Head Start, Job Corps, and the like could be evaluated in terms of their potential for equity maximization.

The less quantitatively but still behaviorally inclined public-organization theorists are likely to move in the direction of Kirkhart's "consociated model." They would move in the direction of sociology, anthropology, and psychology, particularly in their existential versions, while the quantitatively inclined will likely move toward economics, as described above. And, of course, many public-organization theorists will stay with the middle-range theories—role, group, communications, decisions, and the like—and not step under the roof of the grand theories such as the consociated model, the social-equity model, or the so-called systems model.

What does new public administration mean for the academy? One thing is starkly clear: We now know the gigantic difference between "public administration" and "the public service." The former is made up of public-management generalists and some auxiliary staff people (systems analysis, budgeting, personnel, and so on) while the latter is made up of the professionals who staff the schools, the police, the courts, the military, welfare agencies, and so forth. Progressive public administration programs in the academy will build firm and permanent bridges to the professional schools where most public servants are trained. In some schools the notion of public administration as the "second profession" for publicly employed attorneys, teachers, welfare workers will become a reality.

Some public administration programs will likely get considerably more philosophical and normative while others will move more to quantitative management techniques. Both are needed and both will contribute.

The return of policy analysis is certain in both kinds of schools. Good management for its own sake is less and less important to today's student. Policy analysis, both logically and analytically "hard-nosed," will be the order of the day.

Academic public administration programs have not commonly been regarded as especially exciting. New public administration has an opportunity to change that. Programs that openly seek to attract and produce "change agents" or "short-haired radicals" are light years away from the POSDCORB image. And many of us are grateful for that.

Notes

1. An exchange occurring at an informal rump session of the Minnowbrook Conference is especially illustrative of this. Several conferees were discussing errors in strategy and policy in the operations of the U.S. Office of Economic Opportunity. They were generalizing in an attempt to determine how organizations like OEO could be made more effective. Several plausible causal assertions were advanced and vigorously supported. Then a young but well-established political scientist commented that causal assertions could not be supported by only one case. True correlations of statistical significance required an "N" or "number of cases" of at least thirty. The reply was, "Has Public Administration nothing to suggest until we have had thirty OEOs? Can we afford thirty OEOs before we learn what went wrong with the first one? By ducking into our analytical and quantitative shelters aren't we abdicating our responsibilities to suggest ways to make the second OEO or its equivalent an improvement on the first?"

2. Equity is now a major question in the courts. Citizens are bringing suit against governments at all levels under the "equal protection of the laws" clause claiming inequities in distribution. Thus far the courts have taken a moderate equity stance in education and welfare.

2

Social Equity in Context

The essay upon which chapter 2 is based was written in the late 1970s, about ten years after the first Minnowbrook Conference and the publication of the original essay on social equity. By then, the so-called new public administration was no longer new, at least in terms of announcing itself. During the 1970s, there were the beginnings of sorting out of those parts of new public administration that were likely to endure and those that were not. It was also increasingly clear that the word "Minnowbrook" was coming to be the shorthand descriptor for the bundle of ideas and values associated with new public administration and that the phrase "new public administration" was slipping into history; today that phrase is seldom used, replaced by the so-called new public management, a rather different bundle of ideas and values.

By the late 1970s, the social equity perspective in public administration was getting some traction associated with continuing problems of economic, social, and political inequality. The social equity perspective was also advanced by a symposium in the *Public Administration Review.*

Like chapter 1, this chapter presents a multi-theoretical argument based on five models, all of them now very familiar to public administration scholars—the bureaucratic, neobureaucratic, institutional, human relations, and public choice models. The careful reader will have noticed that the five models resemble the theories in the recently published *The Public Administration Theory Primer* (2003), by H. George Frederickson and Kevin Smith. Chapter 1 attempted to build a theoretical structure based on theories of distribution, integration, boundary-exchange, and the socioemotional process. That theoretical structure, or at least its language, has not taken hold. On the other hand, the theoretical language and ideas in Table 2.2 in chapter 2 have endured, many of

Adapted and updated from H. George Frederickson, "The Lineage of New Public Administration," *Administration and Society* 8, 2 (August 1976): 149–74. Used by permission of Sage Publications.

them now built into modern doctrines of public administration (Hood and Jackson 1991).

The theoretical models in both chapters 1 and 2 were designed to describe the linkages between theory and values in the field and how social equity fits into those values. While both approaches are useful, the five models described in chapter 2 have had staying power and do a better job of framing the foundation of values upon which social equity in public administration rests.

❐

The new public administration, of which social equity was originally a part, emerged in the late 1960s and early 1970s as a response to several stimuli, most notably the war in Vietnam, continuing racial unrest, continuing dissatisfaction with the intellectual basis of public administration, and the general shifting going on in the social science disciplines. The four major collections of essays generally identified with new public administration and social equity (Frank Marini's *Toward a New Public Administration* 1971; Dwight Waldo's *Public Administration in a Time of Turbulence* 1971; George Frederickson's *Neighborhood Control in the 1970s* 1973 and "A Symposium on Social Equity and Public Administration" in the *Public Administration Review* 1974) serve to illustrate that there is not *a* new public administration or *the* new public administration. There is, rather, a rich variety of interpretations of what is going on in the social sciences and how that applies to public problems. There is a wide array of values associated with new public administration and social equity, and these values are not always consistent. Therefore, I strongly resist the notion that there must be a single, agreed-upon new public administration with an attendant model that is a complete negation of past theory and norms in the field. This is, then, an argument that what is new in new public administration and social equity flows directly from the values that guided traditional public administration. And new public administration proceeds logically from the aggregation of new knowledge in the social sciences and the focusing of those sciences on public problems. If this is the case, then new public administration and social equity have a rich and significant lineage. A description of this lineage might serve to put new public administration and social equity in context and clarify their objectives.

Political Science

Any consideration of public administration should begin with political science. Clearly, political science is the mother discipline, and almost all of the early American public administration theorists were political scientists

(Woodrow Wilson, W.W. Willoughby, Frank Goodnow, Leonard White, Paul Appleby, John Pfiffner). Political science, and particularly political theory, has traditionally been the locus of the most complete consideration of the normative and philosophical thought that now appears central to public administration. But public administration has always been both more than and less than political science.

In the university, public administration is more than political science in that those who either study or prepare for public administration are more likely to study social psychology and economics than political science. The drift of public administration away from political science is seen in the emergence of schools of public affairs and public policy. We further sense the separation of these fields by the occasional discovery on the part of political scientists that the mother discipline has kept this particular child undernourished and in the corner. But it is the concentration by public administration scholars on theories, constructs, and models from the other social sciences that really marks the importance of the public administration drift from political science. In the government agency, public administration has always been more than political science because the agency is usually staffed by specialists from other disciplines. Few of these specialists have any educational background in public administration, let alone political science. And public administration has always been less than political science, a child of the mother discipline with an uneasy relationship with its mother and a hearty and fruitful search for its "fathers" in the other disciplines.

Most political scientists readily acknowledge the size and power of the bureaucracy. Frances E. Rourke (1976) argues that

> a variety of circumstances in modern life, as, for example, the growing weight of expert knowledge in policy formation, continue to push bureaucracy toward a position of pre-eminence in the governing process . . . this bureaucratic power rests partly on the extraordinary capacities of public agencies as sources of expertise, but partly also on the fact that administrative agencies have become major centers for the mobilization of political energy and support. As a result, bureaucratic politics rather than party politics has become the dominant theater of decision in the modern state. (183–84)

Therefore, it would be logical to assume that bureaucracy would be an important subject to those who study government. Yet the great numbers of men and women employed to carry out government programs—the bureaucrats—are perhaps the least studied actors in American government, at least by political scientists. A recent survey of the research and publishing habits of political scientists shows that only 7 percent of the articles published in political science deal with bureaucracy and the executive branch of government. To understand modern public administration, one must go well beyond political science.

Another way of making the same point is to assert that public administration is not a social science or a discipline but is an application of social science (and other science) to public problems. It is a subject matter, a profession, and a field. Public administration bridges the disciplines and, therefore, takes their relevant parts and applies them to public problems. This is not to say that public administration is not academically or scientifically creative. In fact, it is the bridging and applying function that gives public administration its most exciting intellectual thrusts. The potential for a subject such as public administration to make a scientific breakthrough is at least as great as the potential of the disciplines.

The publication of Thomas Kuhn's *Structure of Scientific Revolutions* (1970) has caused a scurrying to find the paradigm in every field in social sciences. It is intriguing that political scientists not long identified with public administration would take the view that the field is theoretically barren. There are, in fact, five major models in modern public administration, each with its major theorists, empirical referents, postulates, hypotheses, and norms. But most of the research and literature upon which these models are based are not found in political science. The theoretical richness of public administration is noticeably greater than in most other fields of political science primarily because public administration is a "borrowing" field. But the explication and comparison of these theories or models is customarily in the fields from which it borrows: sociology, social psychology, economics, and other disciplines.

The second purpose of this chapter is to discuss and compare these models in terms of values (norms), using values to move beyond empirically supported arguments to arguments found in contemporary political philosophy as to what constitutes good government, ethical behavior, and sound moral reasoning. Values are, therefore, taken to mean the normative suppositions within or underlying the models being discussed and the process of moral reasoning in support of the models. After setting out these models, new public administration is described in value terms, and the lineage between new public administration and the five models is sketched. The third and most important purpose of this chapter is to use the five models as the basis for setting out a theory of social equity in public administration.

Five Models in Public Administration

The five basic models in contemporary public administration are labeled here the classic bureaucratic model, the neobureaucratic model, the institutional model, the human relations model, and the public choice model (see Table 2.1).

Table 2.1

Five Public Administration Models

Theories and Theorists	Empirical Focus (Unit of Analysis)	Characteristics	Values to Be Maximized
Classic Bureaucratic Model	The organization	Structure, hierarchy, control, authority, policy-administration dichotomy, chain of command, unity of command, span of control, merit appointment, centralization	Efficiency, economy, effectiveness
Taylor	The production group		
Wilson	The government agency		
Weber	The bureau		
Gulick, Urwick	The work group		
Neobureaucratic Model	The decision	Local-positivist, operations research, systems analysis, cybernetics, management science, productivity	Rationality, efficiency, economy, productivity
Simon, Cyert			
March, Gore			
Institutional Model	The decision (rational)	Empirical positivist, bureaucracy is an expression of culture, patterns of bureaucratic behavior focusing on survival, competition, technology, rationality, incrementalism, power	Science; "neutral analysis of organizational behavior"; incrementalism; pluralism; criticism
Lindblom	The decision (incremental)		
J. Thompson	Organizational behavior (open systems)		
Crozier	Organizational behavior		
Downs	Individual and organizational behavior		
Mosher	Bureaus and professions		
Etzioni	Comparative organizational behavior (power)		
Blau	Organization behavior (exchanges)		
Riggs	Organization and culture		
V. Thompson	Organizational behavior		

Theorist	Focus		Values
Selznick	Organizational behavior (organismic)		
Human Relations Model	The individual and the work group	Interpersonal and inter-group relations, communications, sanctions, motivation, change, training, shared authority, procedural correctness, consensus	Worker satisfaction, personal growth, individual dignity
McGregor	Supervisor/worker relations		
Likert	Supervisor/worker performance		
Bennis	Behavior change		
Argyris	Behavior change		
Public Choice Model	Organization/client relations and public goods distribution	Antibureaucratic, application of economic logic to problems of public service distribution, highly analytic, market analogues, contracts, smallness, decentralization, bargaining	Citizen options or choices; equal access to services; competition
Ostrom	Decentralized overlapping structures		
Buchanan, Tullock	Public sector as market		
Olson	Client group size and public service distribution		
Mitchell	Distribution		
Frohlich, Oppenheimer, Young	Leadership and goods distribution		
Niskanan	Performance contracting		

The labels are not especially important but are increasingly in common usage, except possibly in the case of what I designate the neobureaucratic model. The theorists put into that category may identify with one of the other categories or will resist being categorized at all. The grouping of theorists is less important (although professionally risky) than the integrity of the five models. In the description of the models and their theoretical and normative characteristics, it will become apparent that although there is an attempt to illustrate the integrity within each model, there are theorists who are really hybrids. Both the research literature and the synthesis literature in each of these models are sufficiently well developed so that it will not be necessary to review them; it is assumed that the reader is familiar with the literature and the major theorists. The consideration of theory and values in these models is done with these caveats.

The Classic Bureaucratic Model

If there is a dominant reality in the practice of American public administration it is the persistence and endurance of the classic bureaucratic model. The bureaucratic model has two basic components: the first, the structure or design of an organization; the second, the means by which persons and work are managed within the organizational design. Max Weber's ideal type is the general beginning point for any understanding of the structural aspects of bureaucracy. In the national government, hierarchy and bureaucracy are seen in the preoccupation with organization charts and the fitting of people into those organization charts (and even having the charts officially signed by "authorities"), along with the elaborate development of job descriptions, personnel classifications, and pay scales. Weber also considered in his description of hierarchy some of the patterns of behavior exhibited by those in scalar organizations, such as the tendency to keep elaborate records, to attempt symmetry in command, and the like.

In its managerial and micro aspects, the classic bureaucratic model begins with Frederick Winslow Taylor's (1985, original 1911) scientific management and can be traced from his initial notions of understanding productivity via time and motion studies to modern-day attempts to measure productivity. In the classic bureaucratic model, structure and management are closely linked. The clearest expression of that linkage is seen in the literature on reorganization. When management or productivity is in trouble, it is standard bureaucratic practice to resort to reorganization, to redesigning the machine, to restructuring. Hierarchy and managerial control are still the existential facts of American public organization. Indeed, Herbert Wilcox (1968) makes compelling arguments based on his research with children that management control and hierarchy are so much a part of Western and particularly American culture that it is very difficult for products of this culture to imagine complex organizations structured in other than scalar ways or managed other than through traditional means of control.

The problem with the classic bureaucratic model was that both practitioners and scholars attempted to make a strict applied science of the design of organization or of the management of organization. The assumption that there was one best way to manage or design a particular organization was obviously faulty. Many of the early attempts to make a science of organizational structure and management were properly criticized by Herbert Simon in his designation of these scientific principles as "proverbs"(1946). But to suggest that there is not or cannot be a strict science of organization design or management is not to suggest that structure and management are unimportant. No one would sensibly suggest a random arrangement of workers, nor would one assume that a product would emerge from a complex organization if there were no means by which workers were caused to arrange themselves in a cooperative and productive fashion. The problem, then, has not been one of developing a science of organizational design or a science of management; it is one of creating designs that are compatible with organizational objectives suitable to workers' needs and desired by the public.

The values articulated by those who developed the classic bureaucratic model are as valid and compelling now as they were fifty years ago. To carry out a public function as fully as possible for the money available (a strict definition of efficiency) is, I would argue, fundamental to any theory or model in public administration. Similarly, carrying out public programs for the least possible money (a strict definition of economy) is equally as basic to any notion of an effective public administration. That an organization should be as productive as possible, that is, providing a quantity and quality of service that matches the expressed needs of a collectivity, is likewise a basic value in public administration.

The values of efficiency and economy are, therefore, a part of new public administration. The problem, then, is not with the values that were to be maximized in the classic bureaucratic models. The problem was in the manner in which it was assumed that efficiency, economy, and productivity could be achieved. Hierarchy, managerial control, authority, and centralization are not as logically linked to the achievement of these values as the early bureaucratic theorists believed. Indeed, much of the work of the organization theorists, who are categorized here as neobureaucratic or human relationists, is about the business of demonstrating that effectiveness, economy, and efficiency are products of relaxed controls, loosened hierarchies, and the breaking down of authoritarian leadership styles.

The Neobureaucratic Model

The neobureaucratic model is one of the products of the behavioral era in social science. The values to be maximized in this model are generally similar to those of the bureaucratic model; therefore the designation "neobureaucratic." In most other respects, the models differ. The bureaucratic model emphasizes structure, control, and the principles of administration, with the unit of analysis usually being the work group, the agency, the department, or whole governments. The values to be achieved are effectiveness, efficiency, or economy. In the neobureaucratic model, the decision is the more common unit of analysis, with the process of decision making being the central focus. The pattern of reasoning is "rational"; that is, decisions are made to achieve as much of a given goal as possible. Modern "management science," systems analysis, and operations research are built on the early writings of Herbert Simon (1957), Richard Cyert and James March (1963). These theorists enriched their work with a deep understanding of formal and informal patterns of organizational control, the limits of rationality, and the like, but the basic modern versions of the neobureaucratic school have stayed with the original means-end logic growing out of logical positivism. The close similarities between means-end analysis of the neobureaucratic model and the policy-administration dichotomy of the bureaucratic model are obvious. The objectives of operations research, systems analysis, policy analysis, and management sciences are essentially the same as those of the bureaucratic theorists. Their work, however, is very sophisticated and contributes substantially to the attainment of efficiency, economy, and productivity.

There could be no better indications of the profound validity of the values that motivated those who designed or chronicled the classic bureaucratic model than can be seen in modern public administration under new banners and rubrics. It is essentially these same values that are being pursued with a marvelous numerical precision in the measurement of productivity. Contemporary public administration is attempting to achieve productivity by methods of measurements rather than by methods of structure and management. To be sure, contemporary approaches are much more scientific and analytically sophisticated, but they still pursue the values underlying the classic bureaucratic paradigm. Modern approaches to policy analysis do enable the administrator or the academic to assess the consequences or results of the operation of public programs more effectively than in the past. But the modern policy analysts and productivity measurers may have as weak a link in their logic as there was in the classic bureaucratic paradigm. If it is erroneous to assume that hierarchy, centralization, and managerial command will achieve efficiency, economy, and productivity, it is probably also erroneous to assume that policy analysis will achieve those objectives. Furthermore, it is probably wrong to assume that either approach is necessarily the friend of democratic or popular control of government. At the same time, it is equally clear that the underlying values of rational decisions to achieve efficiency, economy, and effectiveness are, and always will be, central to any normative dialogue in public administration, and they are certainly central to new public administration. The questions, however, are two: how can one achieve these values, and do these values conflict absolutely with other values that should be central to public administration?

The Institutional Model

The institutional model is a product of the work of many social scientists in the 1940s, 1950s, and 1960s (Perrow 1972). In its basic manifestation, it is more methodologically rigorous than was the work of those who initially described bureaucracy; therefore, its findings will have a stronger empirical warrant. The institutional model is the manifestation of the behavioral era, particularly in sociology and political science.

The concern of the institutional theorist is less with how to design efficient, effective, or productive organizations and more with how to analyze and understand existing bureaucracies. These scholars are generally "positivist" in their perspective, searching for order in complex organizations or for discernible patterns of bureaucratic behavior. Public administration scholars categorized as institutional seem rather less interested in how to make government more efficient, economic, or productive than they are in simply finding out how complex organizations behave.

Within this category fall works such as James Thompson's (1967) remarkable synthesis of organizational behavior, one of the more complete models in modern social science. Frederick Mosher's (1967) analysis and synthesis of the behavior or particular public bureaucratic professional groupings is both empirically and logically rich. Amitai Etzioni's (1961) comparative analysis of complex organizations is equally as complete an integration of the behavioral characteristics of bureaucracy. The "scientists" of the behavioral era have significantly advanced the systematic understanding of bureaucratic behavior. Still there is no agreed-upon model or paradigm, but rather a body of knowledge generally going under the label "organization theory." Public administration scholars are both systematic users of and contributors to organization theory.

If organization theory and the institutional model have been as well developed as is claimed here, what are the normative foundations on which this body of knowledge rests? As is their custom, behavioral scholars simply skirt the normative questions, making the claim that they are in the business of describing organization, not prescribing answers. Yet there are strong normative currents in the institutional model. One of these can be characterized as the school of concerned scholars who have analyzed bureaucracy and discovered it to be powerful, resistant to change, seemingly beyond legislative or executive controls, tending to isolate and seal off its technology and guarantee its sources of revenue, and inclined to concern itself primarily with survival. After having discerned these behavioral patterns, the scholar either observes that bureaucracy is bad and we ought to figure out ways to control it or that this is just a natural phenomenon and the price a complex and advanced society must pay if it wishes government to provide services.

One of the few detailed attempts to defend the values of the institutional model was made by Charles Lindbloom, who argued that rationality is not only unlikely, it is also undesirable. In his *The Intelligence of Democracy: Decision Making through Mutual Adjustment* (1965, he claimed that bureaucracies make decisions in incremental ways, that these decisions are bargains and compromises (really the bargains and compromises of interest group elites), and that they move government gradually toward vague objectives. Further, and most important, this is really the way democratic government ought to work. It is only through incremental decision making that the expertise and skills of the bureaucracy can be integrated with the policy preferences and political biases of elected officials. Those opposed to the incremental view claim it to be nothing more than an elaborate apology for the way an ineffective government system now operates. In the guise of "describing democracy," they reify and justify the weaknesses in democratic systems. In the name of empiricism, they conclude either "That's how things are in complex organizations, and there really isn't much which can be done about it" or "That's how things are in complex organizations, and that's probably how they should be."

The Human Relations Model

The human relations model is in many ways a reaction to the classic bureaucratic and neobureaucratic models. The emphasis in bureaucratic theory on control, structure, efficiency, economy, and rationality virtually invited the development of the human relations movement. Traced to the Hawthorn experiment and to the works of Elton Mayo and his colleagues, this movement has evolved to a highly empirical and strongly researched body of theory in which social psychologists tend to have been the major theorists. Probably the two major works to influence students of public administration have been Rensis Likert's *The Human Organization: Its Management and Value* (1967) and Daniel Katz and Robert Kahn's *The Social Psychology of Organizations* (1966).

The human relations model has its applied manifestations principally in group dynamics, sensitivity training, and organizational development. The emphasis in these training movements clearly reflects the model's underlying values: worker and client participation in decision making, reduction in status differentiations, reduction in interpersonal competition, and emphasis on openness, honesty, self-actualization, and general worker satisfaction. The classic bureaucratic and neobureaucratic models (with the possible exception of the rational decision theorists) clearly are fair empirical representations of public organizations. There is some question, however, as to the impact of the human relations model on government administration. If there has been an impact, it has been slow and slight. This is not to suggest that the empirical findings of human relations theorists are inaccurate; the point is that these findings are based more on experiments and tests than on observations of ongoing complex organizations. Nor is it to suggest that the values on which the human relations movement is based are bogus. However, it does suggest that these values may be in competition with the values on which the classic and neobureaucratic models are based. For example, managerial control and shared authority may conflict, as will efficiency and procedural correctness. Still, the human relations school has provided compelling evidence that under certain conditions shared authority and worker satisfaction are positively correlated with productivity.

The best available description of the clash in values between these models has been done by David K. Hart and William G. Scott (1971). They first describe the remarkable similarities between the classic political theorist Thomas Hobbes and Frederick Taylor, the father of scientific management:

1. Man's nature is essentially evil, slothful, and indolent.
2. This being the case, there must be controls to keep evil men from destroying each other.
3. Preferably, these controls are centralized and autocratic.
4. Although autocratic controls on society (Hobbes) or on the organization (Taylor) result in some loss of liberty, they also result in material advantages, efficiency, and predictability.

Scott and Hart then describe the similarities between the political philosophy of Jean Jacques Rousseau and Douglas McGregor:

1. Men are inherently good, whereas organizations or governments can be evil.

2. Men must overcome their institutions by a new consciousness, the release of emotional strength, and the development of new structures that permit openness, honesty, and authenticity-human relations.
3. New structures are based on a general will or a consensus, and those not conforming must be "trained" to be "free."

Most modern human relations theorists are inclined toward the norms of Rousseau and McGregor, but these norms are not the dominant reality in complex public organizations. Hobbes and Taylor seem to be carrying the day, but the training activities of the human relations adherents may be having some impact.

The Public Choice Model

The modern version of political economics is now customarily referred to as either "nonmarket economics" or the "public choice" approach. This body of knowledge is rich in tradition and intellectual rigor but somewhat light in empirical evidence. Nevertheless, the public choice theorists are having and will continue to have an important influence on American public administration. Vincent Ostrom essentially ties together public choice logic, public administration history and theory, and political philosophy. In his book *The Intellectual Crisis in American Public Administration* (1973), he compares the perspective on public administration developed by Woodrow Wilson, which he labels bureaucratic theory, with the perspectives of the public choice theorist, which he labels a "paradigm of democratic administration." The Wilsonian perspective is, in Ostrom's judgment, a sharp departure from the Hamiltonian-Madisonian perspective on the nature of government. Both, however, trace more directly to the political philosophy of Hobbes. The Wilsonian, or bureaucratic, paradigm has the following components: there will always be a dominant center of power in any system of government; a society will be controlled by that single center of power, and the more power is unified and directed from a single center the more responsible it will become; the field of politics sets the task for administration, but the field of administration lies outside the proper sphere of politics; perfection in the hierarchical ordering of a professionally trained public service provides the structural conditions necessary for "good" administration; and perfection of "good" administration as above defined is a necessary condition for modernity in human civilization and for the advancement of human welfare.

By contrast, the Ostrom interpretation of public choice perspectives, which he bases on *The Federalist*, or Hamilton and Madison, has the following features. The provision of public goods and services depends upon decisions taken by diverse sets of decision makers, and the political feasibility of each collective enterprise depends upon a favorable course of decisions in all essential decision structures over time. Public administration lies within the domain of politics. A variety of different organizational arrangements can be used to provide different public goods and services. Such organizations can be coordinated through various multiorganizational arrangements, including trading and contracting to mutual advantage, competitive rivalry, adjudication, and the power of command in limited hierarchies. Perfection in the hierarchical ordering of a professionally trained public service accountable to a single center of power will reduce the capability of a large administrative system to respond to diverse preferences among citizens for many different public goods and services and to cope with diverse environmental conditions. Fragmentation of authority among diverse decision centers with multiple veto capabilities within anyone jurisdiction and the development of multiple, overlapping jurisdictions of widely different scales are necessary conditions for maintaining a stable political order that can advance human welfare under rapidly changing conditions.

The Ostrom interpretation of the public choice approach may not be universally accepted by public choice theorists, but it is certainly the most theoretically developed argument. The values espoused by public choice theorists are difficult to fault. Citizen choice in services is compelling and can be achieved by moving to the suburban city that has the array of services wanted. But not all citizens have this choice. Competition among jurisdictions or agencies is also enticing, because competition may "tone up" the quality of services generally. But can we afford competition, and if so, how much? If competition enhances efficiency and economy, does it enhance these values for everyone? Have market model applications in the private sector resulted in a wide range of real consumer choices and a high level of organizational productivity? Has the development of collective unionization in the private sector reduced the range of citizen choices and the level of productivity and would the same thing happen in the public sector as unions grow in power?

At the beginning of this chapter, I suggested that the values that guided traditional public administration—efficiency, economy, productivity, rationality—will have a heavy influence on new public administration. The classic, neobureaucratic, and institutional models of public administration emphasize these values and their characteristics. But the human relations and public choice models are departures because they emphasize the values of worker satisfaction, personal growth, individual dignity, and citizens' choice. In the next chapter, I integrate these values with those associated with social equity and set out a model for new public administration.

With this theoretical base, I now turn to social equity.

Social Equity and Public Administration

It is popular to believe that there will be a wilting away of old models in public administration and the emergence of a totally new model. This pattern of theory and model evolution (and devolution) may be common in the life, physical, or natural sciences, as Thomas Kuhn (1970) suggests, but I am of the view that it is not common in the social sciences. My reasons are fairly simple and trace directly to the questions of linkage between theory and value. Public administration is, in many ways, the vehicle for implementing the values or preferences of individuals, groups, social classes, or whole societies. These values are ongoing or enduring, but they are often also competitive. At any point in time, one set of values may be dominant and have a lock on the practice of public administration, as I would contend the classic and neobureaucratic models now do. Therefore, efficiency, economy, productivity, and centralization are dominant norms, and bureaucratic behavior, as well as bureaucratic theory, reflect this domination.

If one can accept these arguments, then concepts of new public administration and social equity would have to begin with the argument that a different (and certainly not new) set of values should predominate. These values would be carried out by organizations that are humanistic, decentralized, and democratic and that distribute public services equitably. New public administration, therefore, would be the attempt to organize, describe, design, or make operative organizations that further these norms. This clearly is a markedly less ambitious interpretation of the objectives of new public administration than many who identify with the field would accept. For example, it is standard practice to call for the "radical reconstruction of public administration" or for the development of a "new paradigm that reorients man." These are catchy notions and often receive unwarranted attention in the academy, where premiums are paid for the freshness of an idea or for being on the cutting edge of "mind-breaking" positions. The critical point is that most of these views are far too utopian to be feasible or so abstract as to be nonoperational. All this is understandable, given the extent to which one takes seriously the label "new." If new public administration scholars or practitioners worried less about whether an idea is old or new and worried more about the extent to which the idea can be operationalized, then it would be possible to develop a truly new public administration. In a very real sense, this is the most radical version of modern public administration because it identifies dominant values and seeks governmental means by which these values can be effectuated.

What, then, can be made of new public administration, both theoretically and normatively? First, new public administration must reject the notion that administrators are value-neutral or administrative theories are value-neutral models. Second, it must be recognized that the values listed in Table 2.1 are legitimate, although often in conflict. If they are in conflict, which values should dominate, given the present American political and administrative situation? And, perhaps more important, which political and administrative adjustments can further the pursuit of these values? Table 2.2 presents a list of values that seem to be a "constellation" of norms or sets of preferences that characterize what appears to concern contemporary public administration. This constellation of values is not at this point a model, but is, rather, the blending of models and values that seem at present to be the most compelling in our political and administrative lives. Not only are they compelling matters in a vague, normative sense, but they also have strong empirical support in modern social science, as well as an excellent basis in contemporary American political philosophy.

For example, an examination of modern social psychology, and particularly as that field bears on administrative behavior and complex organizations, makes it increasingly clear that nonauthoritarian forms of administration correlate with increases in worker morale, satisfaction, and productivity. This aspect of new public administration is, then, little more than an extension of the human relations model.

There is further evidence that when citizens are offered an array of choices with respect to preferred public services, they select those services that they interpret as more responsive to their general needs, which is to say that the broadening of citizen choice equates with the responsiveness of bureaucracies. Again, this flows logically from the public choice model. There is interesting research that indicates that citizen participation and neighborhood control do result in breaking down the dominance of managerial definitions of services that citizens need. Citizen participation and neighborhood control appear to result in a pattern of compromise and adjustment whereby managerial definitions of client needs are adjusted to citizen definitions of their needs. These examples are particularly evident in the field of education, in which citizen participation, neighborhood control, and a general pattern of decentralization are clearly under way. It is also clear from some of this research that there are trade-offs between the values upon which public administration is built. For example, neighborhood control and citizen participation in school decision making probably do result in some diminution in economy and efficiency. This decline in economy and efficiency is, however, offset by an increase in "responsiveness"; the citizens of a particular neighborhood are willing to forego some efficiency, as that term might be defined managerially, for a pattern of services that they prefer, even though that pattern of services may, from a classic public administration point of view, be inefficient. This serves to illustrate that a group of citizens might define a public service as effective

Table 2.2

Values, Structure, and Management in Social Equity

Values to Be Maximized	Structural Means of Achievement	Managerial Means of Achievement
Responsiveness	Decentralization (political and administrative)	Routine client interaction with employees and managers
	Contracting	Managerial definition of democracy, including more than responsiveness to elected officials, but also to interest groups and disorganized minorities
	Neighborhood control over street-level bureaucracies	Training
Worker and citizen participation in decision making	Neighborhood councils with power	Acceptance of an ethic that insists on the right of workers and citizens to participate in those decision processes that affect their lives directly
	Overlapping work groups	Training in organizational development
	Worker involvement in decision processes	
Social equity	Area-wide revenue systems with local distribution systems	Professional codes of ethics spelling out equity
	Public service outputs and outcomes made equal by social class	The managerial commitment to the principle that majority rule does not overturn minority rights to equal public services
Citizen choice	Devising alternative forms of services so as to broaden choice	Reduction of managerial monopoly over a particular service, such as health care or education
	Overlap	
	Contracting	
Administrative responsibility for program effectiveness	Decentralization	Measuring performance, not only on general organizational standards, but also by social class
	Delegation	Measuring performance for whom?
	Performance targets	

in ways that are at rather distinct odds with either managerial or electoral officials' definitions of effectiveness.

If bureaucratic responsiveness, worker and citizen participation in decision making, social equity, citizen choice, and administrative responsibility for program effectiveness are the constellation of values to be maximized in modern public administration, what are the structural and managerial means by which these values can be achieved? Table 2.2 is an attempt to array the alternative means by which it is assumed these values are achieved. This is not to make absolute causal assertions—such as decentralization will bring about responsiveness—it is simply to suggest probabilities, such as that the likelihood of bureaucratic responsiveness occurring seems greater under conditions of political and administrative decentralization. Table 2.2, then, sets out to summarize both the empirical literature (to include case studies and other nonquantitative forms of analysis) and some of the folklore of public administration.

Clearly, the most interesting developments in modern public administration are not empirical but philosophical, normative, and speculative. Most of these are grouped here under the phrase "social equity," which in public administration has emerged as a shorthand way of referring to the concerns and opinions of those who are challenging contemporary theory and practice. As yet, however, the phrase has little substance or precision. Much of the remainder of this chapter will describe, in a summary way, social equity as a positive expression of modern views in public administration. I shall not deal here with the traditional questions of ethics and responsibility in government; these issues will be examined only from the perspective of social equity and new administration. This should not be regarded as a detailed consideration of ethics or morality in public administration. It is designed, rather, to posit a different approach both to theory building in and the practice of public administration.

The problem of equity is as old as government. Dwight Waldo points out that "much governmental action in the United States has not been simply discriminatory but massively and harshly so. Much governmental action has also, however, been directed toward achieving equality; paradoxically, action to assure assimilation and uniformity also has sometimes been insensitive and coercive. Equality," he concludes, "is central to the understanding of much recent and contemporary public administration (1972, 224). It has been seriously suggested that social equity be a standard by which public administrators, both in the bureau and the academy, assess and evaluate their behavior and decisions. Social equity, then, would be a criterion for effectiveness in public administration in the same way that efficiency, economy, productivity, and other criteria are used. The rationale and defense of this criterion are spelled out in some detail here.

Whenever an ethic or standard for behavior is described, it is essential to provide an accompanying caveat. In the present case, the social equity point of view will need to be buffered by a recognition first that there is a high ethical content in most significant public decisions; public problems do not succumb simply to factual analysis. This being the case, if the public servant is to be an interpreter of events and an influencer, if not a maker of decisions, what should be included in the standards of ethical behavior that guide that individual? Surely the standards of ethics and morality that are applicable and sufficient to a citizen in private or social relationships are not adequate for the public decisions of an administrator. And it is now increasingly clear that the decision problems faced by these administrators are seldom black or white in relation to their ethical content and consequences. There often is really no one best way, but instead a decision should be made that maximizes such results as are attainable given the resources available and minimizes negative side effects. And finally, one must accept the proposition that politics and administrative organizations are themselves the best protectors of administrative morality provided that they are open, public, and participatory. Within this context, then, we pursue the development of a social equity ethic for public administration.

Description and Meaning

Having laid out alternative models of public administration and the values each model maximizes, and having set forth primary values in the field, I now turn to the matter of defining and meaning. What is social equity and what does it mean?

What new public administration is striving for is equity. *Black's Law Dictionary* (1957) defines equity in its broadest and most general signification:

> [Equity] denotes the spirit and the habit of fairness and justness and right dealing which would regulate the intercourse of men with men,—the rule of doing to all others, as we desire them to do to us; or, as it is expressed by Justinian, "to live honestly, to harm nobody, to render every man his due." . . . It is therefore, the synonym of natural right or justice. But in this sense its obligation is ethical rather than jural, and its discussion belongs to the sphere of morals. It is grounded in the precepts of the conscience not in any sanction of positive law. (634)

Equity, then, is an issue that we will find to be a question of ethics. We will also find it to be a question of law.

John Rawls, a foremost theorist supporting a concept of equity in government, sets out a splendid framework for a fundamental equity ethic in his book *A Theory of Justice* (1971). When speaking of our government institutions, Rawls states:

> For us the primary subject of justice is the basic structure of society, Or more exactly, the way in which the major social institutions distribute fundamental rights and duties and determine the division of advantages from social cooperation. By major institutions I understand the political constitution and the principal economic and social arrangements. (7)

Justice, then, is the basic principle and is dominant over other principles in Rawls's form of ethics. Rawls begins his theory with a definition of the individual or citizen and states:

> Each person possesses an inviolability founded on justice that even the welfare of society as a whole cannot override. For this reason justice denies that the loss of freedom for some is made right by the greater good shared by others. It does not allow that the sacrifices imposed on a few are outweighed by the larger sum of advantages enjoyed by many. Therefore, in a just society the liberties of equal citizenship are taken as settled; the rights secured by justice are not subject to political bargaining or to the calculus of social interest. (3–4)

In developing his theory, Rawls suggests an intellectual device or technique by which the principles of equity can be set forth. The first and most important intellectual technique is the notion of original position. The original position constitutes an agreement upon the most basic principles of justice upon which all of the basic structures of society (social, economic, and political) will be predicated. The principles of justice that emerge are both final and binding on all: "Since the original agreement is final and made in perpetuity, there is no second chance" (176). In this intellectual condition, it is necessary to have what Rawls calls a veil of ignorance, described as follows:

> First of all, no one knows his place in society, his class, position or social status; nor does he know his fortune in the distribution of natural assets or abilities, his intelligence and strengths, and the like. Nor, again, does anyone know his conception of the good, the particulars of his rational plan of life, or even the special features of his psychology such as his aversion to risk or liability to optimism or pessimism. More than this, I assume that the parties do not know the particular circumstances of their own society. That is, they do not know its economic or political situation, or the level of civilization

and culture it has been able to achieve. The persons in the original position have no information as to which generation they belong. (137)

Obviously, anyone working out rules for social, economic, and political behavior under the concept of original position and with the veil of ignorance would take care to formulate rules that would be acceptable to themselves regardless of their station in society at any time. David K. Hart interprets Rawls this way: "Not knowing specific conditions, they do not know whether they will be among the more advantaged, or the less advantaged. Wisdom dictates, then, that the principles of justice chosen must advance the condition of the least advantaged man, since one could easily be that man" (1974, 14).

To make this theory operative, Rawls then proposes two principles of justice: "The first principle is to have an equal right to the most extensive total system of equal basic liberties compatible with a similar system of liberty for all. The second principle is that social and economic inequalities are to be arranged so that they are both: (a) to the greatest benefit to the least advantaged, consistent with the just savings principle, and (b) attached to offices and positions open to all under conditions of fair equality and opportunity" (135).

These two principles, then, are to be a right of the same significance or order as the present rights as we understand them in government. Hart further states:

> According to Rawls, acceptance of the two principles of justice means that the collective efforts of society would be concentrated in behalf of its less advantaged members. This does not mean that all inequalities would disappear and all good will be equally distributed to achieve parity throughout the society. There would still be disparities in income and status. But there is an irreducible minimum of primary goods (such as self-respect, rights and liberties, power and opportunities, income and wealth) that are due every man, and the minimum must be met. (7)

Rawls states that this is "a strongly egalitarian conception in the sense that unless there is a distribution that makes both persons better off (limiting ourselves to the two-person case for simplicity), an equal distribution is to be preferred" (8).

David Hart argues that self-respect is the most important of the primary goals to which Rawls referred. He writes that "nothing must be allowed to lessen the self-respect in any man, nor may any man be treated instrumentally . . . thus, every social institution or action must enhance the self-respect of every person, whether the least advantaged or most advantaged, since individual self-respect is the foundation of a just society" (8).

It is obvious that Rawls's theory of justice is vastly different from other contemporary patterns of moral reasoning. Rawls does not argue it because it is good or right but rather because there is an increasing importance to the interdependence of persons that makes notions of advantages and disadvantages less and less acceptable. It is a pervasive sense of noblesse oblige or a sense of eternity among people. Rawls states that "in justice as fairness men agree to share one another's fate. In designing institutions they undertake to avail themselves of the accidents of nature and social circumstances only when doing so is for the common benefit" (102). Because not all persons are genetically "equal," the more advantaged have a moral duty to serve all others including the disadvantaged, not for altruistic reasons but because of the significance of human interdependence. As Hart says, "One serves because justice requires it and the result is the continuous enhancement of self-respect. Just actions, then, not only create the optimal condition for human life, they also are a major element in the rationalization of self" (8).

Although all this theory and definition is interesting, we live in a world of large and very complex organizations where the application of such concepts is difficult. This is also a world in which organizations tend to elevate their own needs over individual needs and goals. The problem is one of making complex organizations responsible to the needs of the individual. This requires rising above the rules and routines of organization to some concern for the self-respect and dignity of the individual citizen. Rawls's theory is designed to instruct those who administer organizations that the rights of individuals would be everywhere protected.

Hart summarizes this approach to social equity with the following:

1. The theory of justice would provide social equity with an ethical content. Acceptance of the theory of justice would provide the equitable public administrator with clear, well-developed ethical guidelines which would give social equity the force that it now lacks.
2. The theory of justice could provide the necessary ethical consensus— that the equitable public administrator has both the duty and the obligation to deploy his efforts on behalf of the less advantaged.
3. The theory of justice would impose constraints upon all complex public organizations since no organization would be allowed to infringe upon the basic liberties of individuals.
4. The theory of justice would provide a means to resolve ethical impasses (the original position).
5. The theory of justice would provide a professional code for public administration that would require a commitment to social equity. (9–10)

Stephen R. Chitwood (1974) has given detailed consideration to this subject. An infinite number of patterns that might be used to distribute public services could be reduced to three basic forms: first, equal services to all; second, proportionally equal services to all; and third, unequal services to individuals corresponding to relevant differences.

Equal services to all has, in Chitwood's judgment, limited applicability. In the first place, most government services cannot be equally utilized by all citizens, because services are initially designed to serve the needs of a restricted clientele—compulsory education for younger people, for example. And, of course, there would be insufficient funds to provide all services to all people.

Proportional equality suggests a formula for distribution of services based on some specified characteristic presumably connected to need. For example, the number of uniformed policemen assigned to patrol particular areas may vary according to crime rate. Public assistance may vary according to number of dependents. Chitwood argues that "providing public services on a proportionally equal basis seems both pragmatically and humanistically appealing. On pragmatic ground it provides apparently concrete, objective bases for allocating services among the populace; and on the humanistic side, it allows more services to be provided as their perceived need increases" (30).

In the case of unequal public services, according to Chitwood, individuals receive services in amounts corresponding to relevant differences in some characteristic possessed by those recipients. There are several such criteria. One might be the ability to pay, according to which one would argue that city libraries, parks, and other public facilities be put in the more affluent sections of the city because those citizens pay more taxes. A second criteria would be provision of services on the basis of need, and in this case, parks, libraries, and other public facilities would be located in the less affluent parts of town on the justification that the need is greater there and the citizens living in those regions would be less able to pay to have such facilities. Using this example, it is likely that an equitable public administrator would incline in the direction of need in the distribution of services, at least according to the definitions of social equity set out in the first part of this chapter. It could be further argued that basic or minimum living standards constitute an almost obligatory service to include nutrition, shelter, clothing, health care, employment, education, and other minimally acceptable levels of existence.

Chitwood also sets out the difference between vertical and horizontal equity, both of which are applicable to the three dimensions of equity described above. Vertical equity has to do with criteria for distributing services among heterogeneous people. Under vertical equity, an effort would be made to devise a rationale or criterion for allocating services among differing groups of citizens, say, by sex, age, geographic location, income, and the like. The absence or presence of a given personal attribute, say, wealth, would determine in part the level of services received. Under conditions of horizontal equity, the principle would be to provide equal treatment for equals, say, for example, the annual dollar expenditures for the education of students in the first grade across an entire state would be approximately equal.

Obviously, questions of social equity will be central to future policy decisions in public administration. It is incumbent on the public servant to be able to develop and defend criteria and measures of equity and to understand the impact of public services on the dignity and well-being of citizens. It would follow that concepts of social equity would come to be fundamental in the education of modern public administrators. So, too, will concerns for the responsiveness of complex organizations to the needs of both the individuals working in them and the citizens who are receiving their services. This will oblige the public administrator to be deeply concerned for the social consequences of his or her work. The public servant will very likely be an advocate, but most modern public servants already are. Frequently, however, their advocacy has to do with such public services as fire, police, national defense, environment, and the like. From now on, it will be essential to relate the public servant's substantive field to questions of equity and social well-being. This should cause the administrator to be far more participatory and open in the management of government agencies. It is difficult to know of citizen needs if the administrator is not in direct and routine interaction with elected officials and legislative bodies. Thus, participation and political interaction are critical to the development of the concept of social equity. The public official will come to be understood as a processor and facilitator with elected officials of government response to rapid social, economic, and political change. In fact, an ability to mobilize government institutions to change may well come to define leadership in the future. The public servant will not be a hero or a Don Quixote, but rather a master of mobilizing and distributing public services fairly and equitably when such services are needed and discontinuing them when they are not needed. This does not promise more than can be given, nor does it imply unbridled government intervention. Indeed, just the reverse. The public servant, with elected officials and legislative bodies, will plan the processes of change in a systematic way, keeping front and center a dialogue over what it is that government properly ought to be doing and for whom it ought to be done. Only with such a dialogue can the administrator hope to function rationally.

In their assessment of education for public service, Richard Chapman and Frederic N. Cleaveland (1973) call for the development of a new "public service ethic." The authors do not attempt to define that ethic and suggest, wisely, that it must evolve and must always be a product of the blending of the values associated with public service. The traditional values of public administration—economy, efficiency, effectiveness, responsiveness to elected officials, responsibility—have served us well. But experience indicates that other values (not necessarily new ones) are important to any public service ethic. Certainly citizen responsiveness, worker and citizen participation in the decision process, the equitable distribution of public services, the provision of a range of citizen choices, and administrative responsibility for program effectiveness are values that suit our times. If there is, or even if there ought to be, a public service ethic, these values are as compelling as are the better understood commitments to managerial values.

This is not a negation of the importance of a general public service productivity or of the continuing search for efficiencies and economies in government. It is simply to suggest that the most productive governments, the most efficient governments, and the most economizing governments can still be perpetuating poverty, inequality of opportunity, and injustice. Both the classic bureaucratic model and the neobureaucratic model offer little in the way of offsetting those tendencies. Therefore, modern public administration will search both theoretically and normatively for what Vincent Ostrom (1973) calls "democratic administration."

3

Social Equity

The Democratic Context
and the Compound Theory

The initial conceptualization of social equity in public administration was rather simple and speculative. Not long after publication of the initial essay, it was evident that the application of social equity to public administration needed elaboration. This chapter starts by putting issues of fairness and equity in the broader historical American context. Matters of fairness and equity are at the core of the American public ethos. It is not surprising then that that American public administration reflects the central place of social equity in our public life. What is surprising is that it took so long for social equity to emerge in public administration and to take its place as one of the core values in theory and practice.

The second purpose of this chapter is to briefly describe how and why the concept of social equity is now generally accepted in public administration.

Finally, and perhaps most important, is the presentation of the so-called compound theory of social equity. The claim is that like the other two core values of the field, efficiency and economy, social equity is a complex subject. The compound theory of social equity sets out the categories of equity and the definitions of the primary types. This builds directly on the simpler presentation of the concept of social equity described in Chapter 1.

□

Adapted and updated from the following works: H. George Frederickson, *New Public Administration* (University, AL: University of Alabama Press, 1980), 13–47. Used by permission from University of Alabama Press. H. George Frederickson, "Public Administration and Social Equity," *Public Administration Review* 50, 2 (March/April 1990): 228–37. Used by permission of the American Society for Public Administration.

The question of equality is one of the great themes in the culture of American public life. In the Declaration of Independence and the Pledge of Allegiance, among other significant expressions of American philosophy, the rhetoric of equality permeates our symbols of nationhood. Over and over in our history, from the earliest colonial beginnings, equality has been a rallying cry, a promise, and an article of national faith. So it is that the ideal of equality touches our emotions. All these aspects of equality—protest, hope, and faith, infused with emotion—came together in an August afternoon over a third of a century ago when Martin Luther King Jr. spoke to a multitude at the Lincoln Memorial, repeatedly returning to the phrase: "I have a dream."

Even before the founding of the United States, the people of this continent faced issues of fairness, justice, and equality. Many came to the New World to escape injustice and intolerance and sought to establish justice and equality among themselves—but not between themselves and those who were already here. As they struggled to collectively govern themselves, they experienced unfair treatment at the hands of their colonial masters and rallied to the appeal of the argument, "no taxation without representation"; the subsequent revolution was a fight over fairness and equality.

> We hold these truths to be self-evident, that all men are created equal, that they are endowed by their creator with certain unalienable rights, that among these are life, liberty and the pursuit of happiness. (*The Declaration of Independence*)

> No state shall make or enforce any law which shall abridge the privileges or immunities of citizens of the United States; nor shall any state deprive any person of life, liberty, or property without due process of law; nor deny to any person within its jurisdiction the equal protection of the laws. (*The Constitution*, The Fourteenth Amendment)

At independence and in the constitutional period, there were vexing problems of fairness and equality—including the treatment of our indigenous people, slavery, and the franchise for women. Nevertheless, the broadly based values of equality were so evident among our people that de Tocqueville would write in 1831:

> Among the novel objects that attracted my attention during my stay in the United States, nothing struck me more forcibly than the general equality of conditions. I readily discovered the prodigious influence which this primary fact exercises on the whole course of society, by giving a certain direction to public opinion, and a certain tenor to the laws; by imparting new maxims to the governing powers, and peculiar habits to the governed.

I speedily perceived that the influence of this fact extends far beyond the political character and the laws of the country, and that it has no less empire over civil society than over the government; it creates opinions, engenders sentiments, suggests the ordinary practices of life, and modifies whatever it does not produce.

The more I advanced in the study of American society, the more I perceived that the equality of conditions is the fundamental fact from which all others seem to be derived, and the central point at which all my observations constantly terminated. (De Tocqueville 2003)

Less than a century after our founding, we fought a great war among ourselves over slavery—a profound issue of justice and fairness—and today we continue to struggle with issues of racial justice, fairness, and equality.

Abraham Lincoln said this about the meaning of equality in the Declaration of Independence:

the authors . . . did not intend to declare all men equal in all respects. They did not mean to say all were equal in color, size, intellect, moral development, or social capacity. They defined tolerable distinctness in what respects they did consider man created equal—equal in "certain unalienable rights, among which are life, liberty, and the pursuit of happiness." (Stern 1940, 422)

In the years that followed our Civil War, issues of racial injustice did not recede; indeed, the great scholar Gunnar Myrdal would write *An American Dilemma* in the 1940s, a sobering empirical description of continuing racial injustice and a prescient prediction of its consequences. Then, after the urban riots of the 1960s, the Kerner Commission would issue its report detailing the persistent problems of racial injustice. Finally, in the 1990s, President Clinton assembled a Dialogue on Race in America, a forthright recognition of our continuing struggle with equality, particularly in the context of rapidly changing American demographics. Among the issue considered were the growth of Hispanic and Asian American populations, the aging of America, the increasing presence of women in the workforce, and the potential of those with disabilities.

It might be fairly asked: What does all of this have to do with American public administration? What is the problem?

Justice, fairness, and equality have everything to do with public administration.[1] First, laws do not carry themselves out; that is our work. The early leaders of our field described public administration as the law in action. Second, if public administration implements the law, can we not simply and precisely bring the law to life exactly as it is written? No, because the law is seldom so clear, so precise, so evident that we know how to apply it in one concrete case, and then another, and another. Third, in the early years of our field, it was written that administration should be the neutral implementation of law and policy. We now know better. Public administration is the law in action and involves, indeed requires, interpretation of that law and discretion in its application. Fourth, our public institutions are the settings in which our elected leaders working in our system of democratic self-government struggle with issues of fairness, justice, and equality. But, because public administration is responsible for carrying out their laws and policies, we too have important struggles with these issues. In sum, public administration has much to do with fairness, justice, and equality in American life.

As in our past, there are at present serious problems of fairness, justice, and equality in the United States. We are not as fair, as just, or as equal as we should be, and public administration cannot say that these problems belong only to lawmakers; they are our problems too. And, over the years, public administration has contributed much to a more equitable, more fair, and more just America. And we have much more to contribute.

What Is Social Equity?

It was the efficient and economical management of government agencies that characterized much of the early reasoning in American public administration. Ours was an ethic of management, efficiency, and economy, and we conveniently assumed that its effects would be evenly and fairly distributed among our people. Gradually, beginning in the 1960s, it became apparent that the implementation of many public programs was much more efficient and effective for some than for others. Indeed, it came to be understood that public administration could not logically claim to be without responsibility for some practices that resulted in obvious unfairness or injustice. Based upon this understanding, there emerged an argument for a social equity ethics in public administration, an ethic of importance equaling our ethics of efficiency and economy. Social equity took its place with efficiency and economy as the third pillar of public administration. Indeed, by the late 1990s, a standard text wrote:

> The ethical and equitable treatment of citizens by administrators is at the forefront of concerns n public agencies. . . . Now it is unthinkable (as well as illegal), for example, to deny someone welfare benefits because of their race or a job opportunity because of their sex. Social equity today does not have to be so much fought for by young radicals as administered by managers of all ages. (Shafritz and Russell 2000, 436).

Over the years the phrase "social equality" has come to comprehend the many complex issues associated with fairness, justice, and equality in public administration. In Shafritz and Russell's words:

> Fairness in the delivery of public services; it is egalitarianism in action—the principle that each citizen, regardless of economic resources or personal traits, deserves and has a right to be given equal treatment by the political system. (436)

They then set out three qualities of social equity:

> All public administrators have an obvious obligation to advance social equity. However, this obligation can be legitimately and honorably interpreted in several ways. First is the obligation to administer the laws they work under in a fair manner. It is hard to believe today that this first obligation was once controversial.
>
> The second way of interpreting obligations to advance social equity is to feel bound to proactively further the cause—to seek to hire and advance a varied workforce. The attitude requires a specific approach: It is not enough to go out and find qualified minorities. You must go out, find them, and then qualify them.
>
> The third aspect to advancing social equity is best illustrated by a story. In 1963, George C. Wallace, then governor of Alabama, dramatically stood in the doorway of the University of Alabama to prevent the entry of black students and the desegregation of the university. . . . After a longwinded speech about federal encroachment on states' rights, Wallace stepped aside and [U. S. Attorney General Nicholas] Katzenbach escorted Vivian Malone to the university cafeteria. . . .
>
> After Malone entered the cafeteria, she got her tray of food and sat alone. Almost immediately some white female students joined her. . . . Then, as now, governments can go only so far in forcing social equity. But there is no limit to the amount of inspiration it can provide to encourage people to do the right, decent, and honorable thing. This encouragement has a name. It is called moral leadership. (Carter 2000, 149–52)

Over the years, both the subject of social equity and its language have changed.

Equity is now more broadly defined to include not just race and gender but ethnicity, sexual preference, certain mental and physical conditions, language, and variations in economic circumstances. The words "multiculturalism" and "diversity" are now often used to comprehend this broader definition of social equity.

The phrase "social equity" has taken its place as a descriptor for variables in the analytic constructs of researchers in the field, as a concept in the philosophy of public administration, and as a guide for ethical behavior of public servants. This chapter turns now to philosophical and theoretical issues associated with the application of social equity in public administration and finishes with an elaboration of the so-called compound theory of social equity, including a consideration of some applied aspects of social equity in practice.

Philosophical and Theoretical Developments

As Dwight Waldo (1949) once put it, public administration is the marriage of the arts and sciences of government to the arts and sciences of management. Efficiency and economy are primarily theories of management, while social equity is primarily a theory of government. In the early years of modern American public administration, this marriage, particularly in the conceptions of Woodrow Wilson ([1887] 1941), was balanced. Theories of business efficiency were routinely mixed with theories of democratic government—the argument being that a government can and should be both efficient and fair. However, by the mid-1960s, the marriage had become dominated by management theories and issues, for many years having begged questions of equity and fairness. Even though the general opinion was (and still is) that public administration is part of the political process, there was little interest in developing specifics regarding the ends to which politics and public administration should be put.

Also, in the early years, conventional wisdom dictated that public administration was neutral and only marginally involved in policymaking. Following such wisdom, it was possible to ignore social equity. The current theology holds that public administration is a part or a form of politics, that it often exercises leadership in the policy process, and that neutrality is next to impossible. If that is the case, then it is not logically possible to dismiss social equity as a suggested guide for administrative action that is equal to the values of economy and efficiency.

Initial attempts to return to the marriage of governmental and management questions of equity and fairness were simplistic and superficial. Willbern (1973), in his splendid review of the early literature on social equity, observed that we were "not very precise in defining the goals or values toward which administration and knowledge must be applied" (376). He concluded that "those who wanted to challenge the 'system' and the 'establishment' on grounds of social equity have met with a good many rebuffs and even evidence of backlash but it would probably be a great mistake to dismiss these essays as an expression of a passing mood, an articulation of the particular times in which they were written. On intellectual, analytical grounds, there is something of value and consequence here, a real addition to our faulty and inadequate understanding of human behavior in administrative situations" (378).

So the task was clear: social equity needed flesh on its bones before it could be added to efficiency and economy as the third pillar of public administration.

The process started with a Symposium on Social Equity and Public Administration that appeared in the *Public Administration Review* (Frederickson 1974). In an especially important way, that symposium is illustrative of the theory-building process in public administration.

First, we parsed the subject—in this case, into considerations of social equity:

1. as the basis for a just democratic society,
2. as influencing the behavior of organizational man,
3. as the legal basis for distributing public services,
4. as the practical basis for distributing public services,
5. as understood in compound federalism, and
6. as a challenge for research and analysis. (Frederickson 1974)

Second, after taking a subject apart, good theory-building puts it back together. It is now clear that considerable progress has been made in thinking about, understanding, and applying various parts of the subject. But we have yet to put it back together.

Third, we began the arduous task of definition. Here it is appropriate to turn to the theories of distributive justice. The use of the terms social equity and equality have been essentially without definition in the field. As Douglas Rac and his associates (1981) said, "Equality is the simplest and most abstract of notions, yet the practices of the world are irremediably concrete and complex. How, imaginably, could the former govern the latter?" (3). Yet social equity is to be the third pillar of public administration.

We turn then to a more descriptive theory, for both greater definition and a more likely applicability to the theories and practices of public administration, as well as to its spirit. Following Rae and his associates, we set out both a rudimentary language and a road map for the notion of equality with attendant definitions and examples. We presume to label this construct the compound theory of social equity. In this chapter, it will serve as the basis for later considerations of legal and research perspectives on social equity in the field.

The Compound Theory of Social Equity

The compound theory of social equity comprises types of equality and applications of those types.

Simple Individual Equalities

In individual equality, there is one class of equals for which a single relationship of equality holds. The best examples are the "one person, one vote" principle or the price mechanism of the market-driven economy that offers a Big Mac or a Whopper at a specific price to whomever wishes to buy. The Golden Rule and Immanuel Kant's Categorical Imperative are both formulas for individual equalities. In the practice of public administration, examples of simple individual equality are rare.

Segmented Equality

Any complex society with a division of labor tends to practice segmented equality. Farmers have a different system of taxation from that of business owners, and both differ from that of wage earners. This concept assumes equality within the category (for instance, farmers) and inequality between the segments. All forms of hierarchy use the concept of segmented equality: all five-star generals with comparable seniority are roughly equal to each other, as are all privates first class. Equal pay for equal work is also a form of segmented equality, which is, in fact, systematic or structured inequality. Segmented equality is critically important for public policy and administration because virtually every public service is delivered on a segmented basis—and always by segmented hierarchies. In segmented equality, people are equally unequal.

Block Equalities

Both simple individual and segmented equalities are in fact individual equalities. Block equalities, on the other hand, call for equality between groups or subclasses. In the 1896 *Plessy v. Ferguson* decision, railroad accommodations for blacks and whites could be separate, so long as they were equal. *Brown v. Topeka Board of Education* concluded in 1954 that separations by race were inherently unequal; it required that school services be based on simple individual equality rather than block equality (using race to define blocks). The claims for comparable worth systems of pay for women are, interestingly, an example of block egalitarianism mixed with equal pay for equal work, which is segmented equality.

The Domains of Equality

How do we decide what is to be distributed equally? The domain of equality marks off the goods, services, or benefits being distributed. If schools and fire protection are to be provided, then why not golf courses or other recreational facilities? Domains of equality can be narrowly or broadly defined and have to do with allocations based on a public agency's resources or claims, based on a claimant's demand for equality. Domains of equality constantly shift, aggregate, and break apart. Certain domains—jobs, wages, investments— are largely controlled by the market, while others are controlled primarily by government. Often the governmental domain seeks equality to correct inequalities resulting from the market or from previous governmental policies. Unemployment compensation, Aid to Families with Dependent Children, college tuition grants, and food stamps are all examples of government's practicing compensatory inequality to offset other inequalities outside its domain of allocation but within a broader domain of claims.

Domains can also be intergenerational—for example, should we or our children pay for the federal deficit? (Intergenerational equity is the subject of a later chapter.)

Equalities of Opportunity

Equalities of opportunity are divided into prospect and means opportunity. Under prospect opportunity, two individuals have an equal opportunity for a job if each has the same probability of getting the job. With means opportunity, two people have an equal opportunity for a job if they have the same talents or qualifications. Few examples of pure prospect equality of opportunity exist, but the draft lottery for the Vietnam War came close. In means equality of opportunity, equal rules—such as those for IQ tests, SAT scores, footraces, and so forth—define opportunity. "The purpose and effect of these equal means is not equal prospect of success, but legitimately unequal prospects of success" (Rae et al. 1981, 66). Aristotle's notion that equals should be treated equally would constitute an example of means-based equality of opportunity.

In any given society, not all talent can be equally developed. According to John Scharr, "Every society has a set of values, and these are arranged in a more or less tidy hierarchy. . . . The equality of opportunity formula must be revised to read: equality of opportunity for all to develop those talents which are highly valued by a given people at a given time" (1967, 231; see also Scharr 1964). How else, for example, can we explain the exalted status of rock musicians in popular culture?

The Value of Equality

The value of equality begins with the concept of lot equality, in which shares are identical (similar housing, one vote, and so on). The advantage of lot equality is that only the individual can judge what pleases or displeases him or her. Lots can also be easily measured and distributed, and they imply nothing about equal well-being. The problem, of course, is that lot equality is insensitive to significant variations in need. To remedy this, Rae and associates suggest a "person" equality in which a nonarbitrary rule-based distribution of shares is based on nonneutral judgments about each person's needs. For example, a threatened individual may require more police protection, if police officials so decide, merely to make that person equal to the person who has not been threatened. The same holds true for a child with a handicap compared with one who is able-bodied or for a mentally retarded person versus an individual of average intelligence. An equality that regards the person is often practiced in public administration to make the rules humane.

It is clear that any universal scope for equality is impossible as well as undesirable. Rather than a simple piece of rhetoric or a slogan, the compound theory of social equity is a complex construct of definitions and concepts. Equality, then, changes from one thing to many things, "equalities" (Rae et al. 1981). If public administration is to be inclined toward social equity, at least this level of explication of the subject is required.

Note

1. Throughout this document the phrase public administration is used broadly to include not only the policies and management of governmental and jurisdictional agencies, but the work of nonprofit, voluntary, nongovernmental, and contract organizations with public purposes and engaged in public work.

4

Social Equity and the Question of Administrative Discretion

The essence of Chapter 4 was written in 1996. In public administration, the standard treatment of administrative discretion is based on the Friedrich-Finer debate. Herman Finer (1941) argued that democratic control of bureaucracy was the primary issue and that to ensure democratic government, public administrators should hew close to the law and the regulations and have little discretion in their interpretation. Carl Friedrich (1940) argued that democratic government requires some level of bureaucratic expertise and some considerable latitude in applying that expertise to actual cases. The details of this debate are found in every public administration textbook.

Social equity has much to do with administrative discretion, for without a generous range of discretion, public administration would be considerably inhibited in the practice of social equity. While the Friedrich-Finer debate has to do with administrative discretion, it treats that subject primarily from the perspective of laws and regulations and issues of democratic control of administration. To get issues of social equity in public administration it seemed to me necessary to get a broader treatment of administrative discretion and that meant going to the philosophical bases of the discretion issue searching for its linkages to matters of equity and fairness. Once that has been briefly sketched, I turn to contemporary political philosophy and particularly to the treatment of justice in that literature. Then, because I find their arguments and empirical findings directly germane to the issue at hand, I look at social psychology and its argument that interpersonal and intergroup fairness and equity are the glue that holds society together. All the more reason, it seems to me, that social equity should be the third pillar or value in public administration. Social equity as a third pillar was discussed extensively in Chapter 3.

❏

Adapted and updated from H. George Frederickson, *The Spirit of Public Administration.* (San Francisco, CA: Jossey-Bass, 1997), 97–113. Used by permission of Jossey-Bass.

In American public administration, efficiency and economy have long been the twin pillars of theory. Efficiency—to achieve as much public good as possible for the available dollars—is a compelling rationale for administrative practices. Economy—to accomplish a public goal for the fewest possible tax dollars—is an equally beguiling objective. Much of contemporary public administration, and especially the public choice and policy analysis perspectives on public administration, uses efficiency and economy as the correct measures by which to evaluate policy or assess its implementation.

Evidence shows that concern for equity in public administration did not begin with the advocates of new public administration. Woodrow Wilson provides such evidence in a speech to his followers on election night in 1912: "I summon you for the rest of your lives to work to set this government forward by processes of justice, equity, and fairness. I myself have no feeling of triumph tonight. I have a feeling of solemn responsibility" (cited by Link 1971).

In the early twentieth century, when corruption threatened to overcome the purposes and methods of government, reformers rallied support for efficiency and economy, the more familiar pillars of public administration. While the reformers sought public values that went beyond economy and efficiency, no other values came to be associated with public administration at that time. This was consistent with the view that policymaking and administration were separate functions. The antidote for incompetent and corrupt government was an administrative government concerned with economy and efficiency.

Efficiency and economy were necessary but not sufficient as guides for public administration (Frederickson 1971a, 309–32, 1980). A third pillar of theory, social equity, had to be added to make the field responsive to the needs of the citizens. In his definitive treatment of bureaucracy, James Q. Wilson (1989) wrote: "Equity is more important than efficiency in the management of many government agencies." A governmental program could be very efficient for some citizens yet inefficient for others. And a public program could be economical for some citizens but expensive for others. Without considering the distributive effects of policy implementation, and following a concept of social equity, public administration could neglect the legitimate interests of all citizens.

Although there have been many critiques and evaluations of the argument for social equity as the third pillar of public administration, in this chapter we shall focus on only one. The sharpest criticism holds that public administrators should not have the discretion to use social equity as a guide for policy implementation. To do so would "steal the popular sovereignty" from elected officials who make the law (V.A. Thompson 1975, 66). We demonstrate why administrative discretion is a fact of governmental and nonprofit organizational life, and why social equity should stand with efficiency and economy as guides in the exercise of that discretion.

The Philosophical Beginnings of the Equity-and-Administrative-Discretion Debate

From the Western tradition, we inherit two general philosophical perspectives on the nature of public administration: administering society's public decisions and allocating its public resources. The two perspectives differ as to how public decisions shall be applied in practice by administrators. One approach argues that no problem of administrative discretion exists—that administrators can neutrally and successfully apply the law, and that they actually make no decisions regarding public resource allocation; they merely carry out the laws and regulations. The other approach recognizes the ambiguity of administrative discretion and the fact that administrators depend on substantive norms (values) to guide their interpretation of law and their allocation of resources. This tradition proposes that equity be the value that guides officials in their decisions. Plato has been associated with the first approach, Aristotle with the second.

The debate in the Western tradition over the role of public officials revolves around application of the law, and it dates to a disagreement between Plato and Aristotle over the role of judges. In the Platonic approach, courts can simply and clearly apply laws (Plato 1970 trans.). The Aristotelian approach argues that this is impossible in principle, because every application of a law involves further elaboration of that law, and elaboration of law without reference to equity results in injustice (Aristotle 1962 trans.).

The Platonic-Aristotelian debate over the nature of legal interpretation can clarify the issues facing modern public administration. We argue, as Aristotle did, that to administer laws without reference to social equity results in injustice; equity must therefore be recognized as fundamental to the practice of public administration. This means that developments in the Aristotelian-Platonic dialogue may be applied faithfully to discussions of public administration's role in society. We survey these developments here.

Attempts to define precisely and limit severely the role of public administrators fall within the Platonic tradition or legal theory. Plato created a dichotomy between integrity to the general law on one hand and the application of justice in the particular case on the other. He maintained that using "justice" as a criterion for interpreting the law in particular cases required absolute wisdom and knowledge on the part of the judge. Since absolute wisdom about the nature and application of justice is, of course, an impossible quality in mortal judges, Plato sacrificed justice in these particular cases for adherence to law in its general form. Plato defined the issue in terms of a choice between perfect, abstract justice and imperfect but stable human law. Since most people recognize that perfection is impossible, we naturally agree with Plato if we accept his definition of the issue.

Aristotle did not accept Plato's definition. He argued that people choose not between perfection and stability but rather between various possible ways of approximating justice in society. In administering any general law, officials will necessarily encounter some questions that legislators simply could not have anticipated when they formulated the law. Public officials (judges, in Aristotle's framework) are, in principle, always faced with discretionary decisions about how to proceed. Aristotle argued that public officials must continually choose between various possible ways of reaching justice in the particular administrative decisions they confront. The issue for Aristotle is practical rather than ideal and theoretical: How can officials reach the most practically just decisions?

To simply follow the law, as Plato suggests, is not an adequate answer when an unexpected case arises. Aristotle argued that what the law demands should be interpreted in light of the more general goal of justice, which the law was meant to approximate. Thus justice, Aristotle argued, is of two kinds: legal justice and equity justice. Legal justice results from applying a law that is clearly and undoubtedly interpretable in its requirements. Equity justice characterizes cases in which the application of a law depends on substantive principles (the spirit of the law) to resolve ambiguity. It also characterizes cases in which legal justice would result in substantial injustice. Aristotle therefore argued that the equitable is superior to the just; to apply the law without regard for equity results in injustice, not in the best approximation of justice, as Plato claimed.

A further implication of Aristotle's argument is that (contrary to Plato's assumptions) administrators can never neutrally apply the law, for two reasons. First, legal justice is not neutral in cases calling for equity justice, in which strict adherence to the written law is decidedly unjust. Second, in many cases, what the law requires in all its details is not so completely clear that only one interpretation is possible. Officials always use some interpretation of the law rather than following it to the letter, because its ambiguity forces them to do so. However, in Aristotle's approach, officials should be criticized if their interpretations of the law are not based on reference to the principles of justice lying behind the law.

What are the implications of these arguments for public administrators? Plato would prefer that public officials simply apply the law as it is written. But if Aristotle is right, what is simple about applying the law? Aristotle would have officials interpret the law with regard to its spirit as well as to equity.

But if Plato is right, by what shared standards can officials' interpretations be limited once they have crossed the line from application to interpretation?

These questions are precisely those facing public administrators in the modern state, who are charged with fulfilling particular mandates that vary with their position. Administrators may be responsible for administering a public school system or a city budget or a snow removal system. In each position, the administrator's mandate is defined by an enabling statute, a city code, or some other authoritative statement. The Platonic argument is that public officials should simply follow the statute or other authorization to fulfill their mandate. The only additional guidelines that administrators need, this tradition argues, are the principles of efficiency and economy—which, in turn, are merely the rational corollaries of any authoritative mandate and do not really add any demands beyond the mandate. Efficiency and economy simply guide administrators toward the best means of fulfilling their responsibilities.

In the Aristotelian argument, on the other hand, the mandate of the public official can be understood only in light of its spirit. The mandate—the actual written words directing the administrator—never so clearly defines what the task is that the administrator can act as a machine, efficiently and economically doing the job. This argument suggests that officials must have an understanding of the spirit of the mandate to guide them as they make the inevitable discretionary decisions. This understanding, according to the Aristotelian tradition, should incorporate the principle of equity, which is a concern for justice that varies appropriately by situation.

We now can clarify several issues that need resolution. First, which tradition—the Platonic or Aristotelian—is more appropriate as a guide for modern public administrators? We argue that the Aristotelian approach is more appropriate, and we will defend that choice. Second, do administrators acting under the Aristotelian framework illegitimately usurp power from democratically elected officials? They do not. Third, what does equity within the Aristotelian tradition really mean? How can we give determinacy to the general notion of equity? Does equity mean the same thing for all administrators in all positions? Is it a process or an outcome value? To help answer these questions, we look to developments in philosophical analysis, in social-psychological theory, and in the American political tradition itself.

Dworkin and the Necessity of Principle in Law

Ronald Dworkin distinguishes between the "rule-book" and "rights" conceptions of law (1985, 11–15), a distinction that parallels the disagreement between the Platonic and Aristotelian traditions on the role of equity for public officials. While Dworkin's discussion applies most directly to judges, it is relevant to our discussion of equity in public administration. Most important, the rule-book concept of law is exactly the one held by theorists in the Platonic tradition, and Dworkin shows clearly why that concept is wrong. We differ with him on the issue of exactly which theory should replace the rule-book concept, because we are developing a theory for public administrators not judges.

The rule-book concept of law holds that the requirements of law are spelled out somewhere in written statutes or case law, and that those requirements, at least in principle, could be brought together in one clearly stated book of rules. Thus, legal requirements are those—and only those—that appear in the rule book; if some supposed requirement or right is not listed in the stated rules, it does not exist. The rule-book concept has an affinity with democratic rule, because under this conception only elected legislatures have the authority to add new rules to the rule book or to take others out—a strict application of the policy-administration dichotomy.

The problems with the rule-book conception of law arise, Dworkin argues, most sharply in "hard cases," in which a dispute occurs over what the correct decision should be. Hard cases arise not because there are no rules that relate to the case—in modern law, rules relate to almost any situation—but rather because the rules that relate to the case at hand either are ambiguous or present several possible interpretations in the concrete situation. Hard cases in law are analogous to a public administrator's practical everyday questions about fulfilling his or her mandate, which is never so completely clear that he or she can simply act mechanically. The administrator always needs some guidelines for fulfilling the mandate; economy and efficiency are the traditional ones.

The rule-book conception of law proposes several suggestions for judges to use in deciding hard cases; these suggestions attempt either to make the decision as mechanical as possible or, when that is impossible, to allow the judge to use personal policy preferences to resolve the issue. These rule-book solutions parallel the standard public administration reliance on efficiency as a guide to interpreting the administrator's mandate, and they beg crucial questions, just as the efficiency argument begs the question "Efficient for whom?"

When the application of a law is unclear, the rule-book position is that judges should use the intent of the legislature to decide the issue. Dworkin points out, however, that apart from the practical difficulty of determining that intent, there is a significant problem in principle with the idea of intent. Intent can never give an unambiguous solution to an ambiguous hard case, because the majority that passes a law is always composed of a number of factions, each with its own intent. In addition, each faction (or even each individual) has several layers of intent, from vote seeking to public policy preferences.

An appeal to legislative intent to determine the application of a law is always ambiguous and always involves interpretation.

The rule-book approach to law acknowledges that in rare cases no clear answer will be found and that the judge must then make an independent decision based on his or her policy preferences. This approach provides two polar alternatives for judges: either they mechanically apply the law as it is written or, when this is impossible, they are free to act on their own personal preferences.

Dworkin provides a third alternative between the option of neutral application and the democratically questionable option of personal preferences. He argues that judges should make judicial decisions based on their understanding of the spirit behind the letter of the law. Under Dworkin's alternative, judges should interpret based on their relatively coherent overall understanding of what principles the legal tradition as a whole embodies. The interpretation is limited by the community's shared concepts of these principles and by the historical tradition of the community. Such principles provide coherent guidelines for judges when they must decide how to interpret law in a unique case; that is, judges do have guidelines for defining justice in particular cases, and they do have guidelines for defining equity in cases in which legal justice would produce substantial injustice. In Dworkin's view, then, application of the law is inherently political but not personally preferential.

There are obvious difficulties in applying Dworkin's argument directly to public administrators. While Dworkin's devastating critique of the rule-book concept of law applies directly and usefully to the standard Platonic concept of the public administrator's mandate, Dworkin's suggestions for how judges should decide cases are inappropriate for public administrators. Public administrators are not judges, and the discretionary situations they face are not cases. The Aristotelian tradition, however, provides an alternative concept that avoids the pitfalls of the rule-book notion of the administrator's mandate.

To avoid the muddles of both neutral application and unbridled personal preference, Dworkin proposes that judges base their legal interpretations on their understanding of the spirit of the law. Public administrators, on the other hand, can avoid the two unacceptable options by recognizing the principle of equity and by engaging the citizens they serve in a dialogue about the appropriateness of their mandate.

Lowi, Gruber, and Modern Platonic Public Administration

Both Aristotle and Dworkin recognized the problematic nature of administrative discretion and proposed methods of tying discretionary decisions to the public interest. Theodore Lowi (1969) proposes a very different solution—a modern administrative Platonism. He attacks the institutional nexus between the administrative state and interest-group politics, and he notes that the expansion of the administrative state is connected to an expansion of administrative discretion. Unable or unwilling to make difficult and controversial policy decisions, Congress has delegated many of those decisions to administrative agencies. Congress has given vague and general authorizations of power to these agencies, which now govern in conjunction with interest groups. In Lowi's view, the broad discretion of administrative agencies, coupled with the influence of interest groups in the administrative process, violates the public interest and denies the rule of law.

Lowi's solution is to limit administrative discretion by "restoring the rule of law" (297). To accomplish this, the Supreme Court should reject as unconstitutional all broad and vague authorizations of power by Congress to administrators. The result would be, Lowi hopes, a transfer of administrative decision making back to Congress and a diminution of administrative discretion. Like Plato, Lowi would attempt to prescribe for administrators exactly what they may do to fulfill their mandate.

But also like Plato, Lowi fails to recognize that proliferation of authoritative rules does little to harness administrative discretion; every rule itself requires interpretation. As John Dewey noted in the early twentieth century, the proliferation or laws reflects a breakdown of public spirit but does nothing to revitalize that spirit (Dewey 1930, 73). Administrative discretion is harnessed to the public good not by more rules but by appreciation of the spirit of the law and its relation to the public good. Ways of revitalizing that spirit must be found, but they will not be found by passing more laws, no matter how clear. Modern arguments about the need to rebuild our civic capital (Putnam, Leonardi, and Nanetti 1993) and the extreme applications or the law that are criticized in *The Death of Common Sense* (Howard 1995) suggest that the answer does not lie in more laws or in a bureaucracy that can implement the law only in a strict and narrow sense.

Judith E. Gruber, noting the growth and power of public administration, shares Lowi's diagnosis but proposes a different cure (Gruber 1987). Instead of making laws that are more precise, and creating a "juridical democracy," the discretion of public administrators should be controlled by the theory of exchange. "In an exchange model, control results not from political actions telling bureaucrats what to do but from constructing conditions in which bureaucratic behavior is constrained in exchange for resources that bureaucrats seek" (211). Gruber then refers to stringent budgetary controls to "strip recalcitrant administrators of their funding and, in some cases, of their jobs."

Under certain circumstances and at certain times, Gruber's cure works. It does not, however, cure the use of administrative discretion. It uses a false argument about bureaucracy and administrative discretion to cure ailments that have to do with policy disagreements and the exercise of political power. For example, the Reagan administration preferred the dismantling of many federally funded domestic programs that were carrying out what Congress had authorized and funded. Were those programs "out of control" or exercising unwarranted administrative discretion? Probably not. It was simply easier and more politically effective to use rhetoric about bureaucratic bumbling, waste, and red tape than to address the policy issues more directly. Many of the domestic programs formerly administered or funded by the federal government are now operated by state and local government—by public administrators who must exercise discretion in carrying out policy. Exchange theory can certainly explain how budgeting control can diminish or even eliminate a particular public program. But it cannot explain why the bureaucracy or the exercise of administrative discretion is defined as the problem when, clearly, the problem is a debate over what should be done in American government, at what level in the federal structure, and by which agencies (J.Q. Wilson 1989).

Equity as Process

The means of revitalizing the public spirit for administrators can be developed by consulting Aristotle and Dworkin. Plato argued that judges should simply apply the law because to do more—to interpret the law based on a standard such as equity—seems to cross the line separating neutral expertise from political bias. Dworkin and others argue persuasively, however, that even (or especially) neutral expertise is subject to political bias, which is all the more egregious because it is not open to public evaluation. Dworkin suggests that we choose not between neutral application and political interpretation, but between hidden and publicly open political interpretations. Thus, he suggests that judges should carefully, coherently, and publicly elaborate their political theory in their decisions and opinions.

But public administrators need a different method of making their decisions open before the public. As noted earlier, administrators are not judges; they do not make autonomous decisions and then present the formal reasons for those decisions. Aristotle dealt with this problem as well; he, too, was concerned about making official decisions nonarbitrary, even when those decisions are not directed completely by the written law.

Aristotle suggested that equitable decisions develop most fully from public dialogue among friends and equals. For Aristotle, friends are those engaged in the same social practice and who, as a result, know the ins and outs and the risks and benefits of that social practice. Equals are those who have the same rights and responsibilities for decision making and participation in a political community. Aristotle argued that only friends and equals are in a position to understand the issues related to equitable public decision making; friends and equals, through dialogue, can decide what is equitable for different members of their community. He denied the possibility of defining in objective, neutral, universal terms what equity would mean across a variety of issues. Equity, according to Aristotle, can be determined only through political dialogue within a political community. This position is remarkably similar to contemporary concepts of networks and governance.

Public dialogue between friends and equals is a high standard if applied to the process of administering government and its programs. But if the process of administration is political, as thinkers from Aristotle to Dworkin have argued, then some means must be found to make administration nonarbitrary from the standpoint of the public.

One approach that attempts to remain faithful to the Aristotelian tradition of dialogue between friends and equals suggests that those citizens affected by public administration decisions should be included in public dialogue about the nature of those decisions. This is the participatory-process or citizen-participation approach (Frederickson 1982), which suggests that public administration decisions will be equitable if the process used to reach them is fair. The process is fair if all affected citizens are given a real voice in the development of the decision. The participatory-process approach also stresses that the equitable outcome of administrative decisions is not the only benefit of such a process. Fair participatory processes are thought to cultivate educated, active, and virtuous citizens. This approach, like Aristotle's, emphasizes that by our methods of governing and administering we create not only our public policies but ourselves.

The participatory-process approach has obvious virtues; it has several weaknesses as well. Some administrative decisions involve such technical and complex issues that only with great difficulty and much time could the affected citizens understand, much less participate in, the decision-making process. This technical complexity is part of the nature of some issues and is not merely part of some plot to keep citizens uninvolved; to make that charge is naive and distinctly unhelpful. To respond equitably within a technically complex context requires principled thought and responsible action. John Rawls's *A Theory of Justice* (1971) can provide guidance here.

Although Rawls intends to provide a theory of justice for all societies, his approach is particularly applicable for a large, complex society like our own. He argues that social structures and social policies should be so constructed that whatever inequalities they allow favor the most disadvantaged group. Rawls reaches this conclusion by suggesting that if any of us were placed in an "original position" without knowledge of our particular place in society (among other things), we would choose such a principle to guide the construction of social structures and policies. We would do so because if we were to end up in the least advantaged group, we would want the society so constructed. Rawls's argument uses our own rational self-interest to encourage us to take the position of disadvantaged groups and sympathize with them.

The significance of Rawls's approach for our purposes is that it provides a structure for discussing the demands of an equity principle in those situations in which technical complexity precludes an actual dialogue between public administrators and the citizens they serve. This approach encourages public administrators to notice particularly the effects of their actions on disadvantaged groups in society and also to take the position of those disadvantaged groups in official dialogue over the development of administrative decisions.

The insight of both Aristotle and Rawls—that equity and justice have a participatory and dialogical nature—has been recognized for some time by those associated with the so-called new public administration, whose advocates have argued that equity in the practice of public administration can be determined only through the participation of affected citizens. Administrators, in this view, must work to include disadvantaged groups in the dialogue on administration and must at times take the position of those groups (Marini 1971; Frederickson 1980, 1990b).

Equity and U.S. Public Administration

Dwight Waldo (1990) points out that we have called upon government to assume more and more societal functions. Waldo writes that the "core" state-serving military, legal, and economic functions has been greatly expanded. Furthermore, he writes, it is now possible to "speak meaningfully of the Service State, the Promotional State, the Regulatory State, and the Welfare State" (38). But recent trends have gone even further: "I raise now the question whether we are now trying to add another function, another level—another state. This might be designated the Redistributive State or, better, the Equity State. My point is that recent years have seen an increase in programs that go beyond welfare as that has been traditionally conceived, programs that seek more directly to achieve intangibles indicated by words such as freedom, equality, and justice; and beyond these, such 'nonpolitical' words as dignity and fulfillment" (39).

Increasingly, the courts are concerned with public organizations' observance of the legal and constitutional rights of their employees, clients, and charges. David Rosenbloom (1983) addresses these specific issues squarely by examining the judicial response to the rise of the administrative state. He argues that the rights of individuals, employees, clients, and "captives" (prisoners and those confined to public mental health facilities) have been greatly expanded by judicial action. The courts have imposed judicial and constitutional values upon areas where administrative values such as efficiency and economy formerly reigned supreme. Rosenbloom argues effectively that the courts have forced public administrators to add terms such as due process, equal protection, right to treatment, right to habilitation, and constitutional standards to their lexicon of administrative values. In short, "judges have sought constitutionality, not efficiency or economy" (51–55). Court involvement in the financing of public schools in many states and in public mental health facilities in Alabama and New York and in virtually all of the state prison systems suggests that the courts are not merely making idle threats. What the courts have imposed are not matters for ethical reflection but values that must be incorporated into the way that public administrators approach their jobs. These values cannot easily be swept away in the name of economy or efficiency.

Equity is given second billing in public administration, often being preceded by the phrase "efficiency or . . ." (Wilensky 1981). In the past, as Wilensky makes evident, the focus of equity considerations was on outcomes and distributional effects, while efficiency matters were considered issues of process. Equity considerations dealt with programs' goals of redistribution or with providing basic services and outcomes in an equitable (that is, fair) way; equity-efficiency debates compared outcome and process values. Equity values emerging from constitutional developments and from trends in political theory are now emphasizing process values in addition to outcomes.

Equity as Social Glue

Social psychology contributes two insights to emphasizing the role of equity in administering social rules. First, a shared conception of equity is one element that enables groups to cohere—it defines fairness for a group and thus provides a framework for resolving disagreements over the allocation of value. Second, differences in the power of various participants are an important factor in defining equity.

Social psychologists have not only a definition but an entire theory of equity. Walster and Walster (1975) state their equity formulation as follows: "In general terms, two people are in an equitable relationship when the ratio of one person's outcomes to inputs is equal to the other person's outcome/ input ratio. Inputs are defined as 'what a person perceives as his contributions to the exchange,' for which he expects a 'just return' . . . outcomes are the individual's 'receipts' from a relationship" (21).

Walster and Walster note that, depending on the situation, different societies at different times will consider different inputs to be relevant to considerations of justice. They argue, however, that the same theoretical framework—equity theory—predicts "when persons will feel equitably or inequitably treated and how they will respond to their treatment" (26).

The importance of social-psychological equity theory for public administration is made clear by Walster and Walster's summary of the theory's second proposition: "Groups can maximize collective rewards by evolving accepted systems for 'equitably' apportioning rewards and costs among members; thus, members will evolve such systems of equity and will attempt to induce members to accept and adhere to these systems" (30).

Equity theorists argue that equity is the glue that holds groups together, that feelings of inequity engender distrust, and that the response to inequity predictably results in declining legitimacy of the regime.

Equity frameworks in social groups are not without a basis in power, however. Walster and Walster argue that those who wield power in a group are able to capture a disproportionate share of community goods and persuade others to acknowledge the equity of unbalanced allocation. Equity standards in social groups, according to this view, are partly the result of power struggles over the definition of values.

Conclusions

The Platonic ideal of the standards that govern public administration—neutrality, efficiency, and economy—is a myth. Thinkers from Aristotle through Dworkin and Rawls show the weaknesses and dangers of that ideal. The problem that public administrators face is how to formulate and put into practice a valid alternative ideal that emphasizes responsibility to the public but avoids the myth of neutrality. Such an ideal will recognize the political nature and political biases of any standard that public administrators might use to guide their decisions. It will therefore emphasize the value of a fair process for reaching administrative decisions.

Aristotle, Dworkin, and Rawls provide different conception of processual fairness, each suitable for different aspects of the administrator's job. Aristotle emphasized the importance of dialogue between friends and equals to derive equitable standards, while Dworkin emphasizes that decisions made by autonomous administrative processes must be as publicly open as possible, with full disclosure of the reasons behind the decisions. Rawls's theory suggests that issues too complex and technical for actual dialogue between citizens and administrators may still be resolved equitably by administrators who take the role of disadvantaged groups in the decision-making process. If the Platonic ideal of neutrality, efficiency, and economy is too often a mask for real political biases, as Aristotle maintained, then the philosophical and legal positions we have developed here are the primary responsible alternatives.

Because the concept of social equity is often associated with social liberalism, it is fair to say that concerns about equity have not been particularly salient in the past few years. The consistent opposition of the Reagan and George W. Bush administrations to affirmative action efforts through the Justice Department stands as perhaps the clearest indication, but other examples can be found as well. The transformation of health policy considerations from concern about access to almost total preoccupation with cost containment furthers the point. The Clinton administration brought the access issue—which is essentially an equity issue—back to the policy table. And with the Obama administration, the health equity issue is back again.

At the federal level, massive deficits have now forestalled even discussion of major social programs that address equity issues. State and local governments have been forced to scramble to make up for reductions in federal dollars, thus limiting their ability to maneuver. When governments suffer from fiscal scarcity, their tendency is to cut down to their core functions—to eliminate programs and aspects of programs that are not considered absolutely essential. The willingness of scholars in public administration to embrace cutback management, privatization, and third-party government indicates a lack of concern for those at the bottom of the economic ladder.

Clearly, the organizational and political environments are still not conducive to the flowering of social equity in practice. However, some theoretical and empirical progress has been made, and some programs have been established with the specific purpose of dealing with equity problems.

Aaron Wildavsky (1988) summarizes the present condition of public administration by describing the organizational environment as one of ubiquitous anomie. He then links the condition to ideological dissension in the political environment and concludes that public administrators are headed for difficult days. What better time to consolidate normative considerations into a single value? Social equity is the most frequently listed public administration value besides economy and efficiency. It is a residual value that stands for a cluster of considerations that must always be addressed.

Embracing equity as the third normative pillar of public administration requires public servants to seek out and work toward more just allocations of public goods and services, to represent those who do not otherwise have access to public policy processes, to seek the public interest or greater good, and to respect the dignity of individuals (public employees as well as other citizens) and tirelessly safeguard their rights.

Public administration should not be deterred by the complexity of the social equity concept. Economy and efficiency have not been without some theoretical confusion and yet have served us well as guides. The fact that pursuing equity requires more energy and reflection than pursuing economy or efficiency may simply come from our status as political descendants of Machiavelli. John Rohr wrote *Ethics for Bureaucrats* (1989) in response to his assessment of modern humankind's moral condition. In the book he states: "When Machiavelli told us to look at the way things are and not as they ought to be, he made us modern men; but in so doing he bequeathed us a sorry legacy of trained incapacity for sound moral argument" (3).

Rohr proposes that, as a remedy for trained incapacity, a study he conducted of regime values, including equality, as found in Supreme Court decisions. His structured meditations on the values of equality represent an alternative to the proactive pursuit of a vague norm of social equity.

Perhaps more theory building—and a bit more practice in grappling with equity issues—will in time make the subject less formidable. It is time now to consolidate our understanding of the concept of social equity and shore up its place as a pillar of our field.

5

The State of Social Equity in American Public Administration

Unlike chapter 1, which was written in 1969, and chapters 2, 3, and 4, much of which was written in the 1970s and early 1980s, chapter 5 was written in 2005. It is, therefore, far more historical and reflective than the earlier chapters. I discarded several alternative titles for this essay in favor of the rather bland "State of Social Equity in American Public Administration." Upon further reflection, and in the interest of a title that is somewhat more descriptive of the tenor of the chapter, today I would probably use a title like "Social Equity in Public Administration: Succeeding in Theory, Struggling in Practice." The point of this alternative title is that social equity is now broadly accepted in academic and theoretical public administration, as the chapter claims. However, the application of social equity in administrative practice is very complex and challenging. As the chapter points out, applications of social equity to the street-level practices of public administration are freighted with ethical issues. Indeed, a reading of chapter 5 should make clear that social equity is a theoretical perspective on public administration, a set of prescriptions to guide the practices of public administration, and an ethic—the social equity ethic.

Chapter 5 completes a general summary of the history and evolution of social equity and public administration. The next three chapters are more detailed and specific considerations of social equity applied to intergenerational equity, law and research, and public education.

◻

Over the years, public administrators have contributed much in helping to create a more equitable, fairer, and more just America. Yet we have much more to contribute. As a core value in public administration, social equity is

---

Adapted and updated from H. George Frederickson, "The State of Social Equity in American Public Administration," *National Civic Review* 94, 4 (Winter 2005): 31–38. Used by permission of Jossey-Bass.

no longer novel or new. Nevertheless, during the past forty years, as social equity has grown in importance in public administration, there is an irony: Americans have become less equal in virtually all aspects of social, economic, and political life. In our literature, in our classrooms, and in our administrative practices, we have learned to talk the social equity talk. But if the data on the growing gap between the haves and have-nots in American are any clue, we are not walking the social equity talk. In this essay, I attempt to describe the changing terrain of public administration and sketch the challenges administrators face as they navigate both the theory and the reality of that terrain. Finally, I offer some suggestions for walking the social equity talk in the years ahead.

The Evolution of Social Equity in American Public Administration

In his seminal essay of almost a century ago, "General Principles of Management," Henri Fayol listed equity as one of fourteen general principles. His description of equity was entirely internal, having to do with equitable or fair treatment of employees. Fayol put it this way: "Desire for equity and equality of treatment are aspirations to be taken into account in dealing with employees. In order to satisfy these requirements as much as possible without neglecting any principles of losing sight of the general interest, the head of the business must frequently summon up his highest faculties. He should strive to instill a sense of equity throughout all levels of the scalar chain" (58).

Though claiming equity to be a primary principle of management, Fayol did not consider the details of how to achieve equity in the context of the "scalar chain," or hierarchy, which contains such obvious inequalities as difference in pay, authority, and responsibility. Furthermore, because his founding essay had primarily to do with business organization, Fayol did not wrestle with the unique public administration challenges of equity in public policy or service delivery. Except for an essay by Woodrow Wilson, none of the other founding documents consider what we now call social equity in public administration.

Wilson pointed out that it is "harder to run a constitution than to frame one" and claimed that "administration lies outside the proper sphere of politics"; nevertheless, he describes a form of public administration social equity. Consider these words from his founding essay, "The Study of Administration" ([1887] 1941): "The ideal for us is a civil service cultured and self-sufficient enough to act with sense and vigor, and yet so intimately connected with the popular thought, by means of elections and constant public counsel, as to find arbitrariness or class spirit quite out of the question" (24).

Aside from these glancing blows, and the more considered treatment of justice in the early literature, for the first several generations of the field of public administration it was simply assumed that good administration of government was equally good for everyone. It was during the 1960s that it became increasingly evident that the results of governmental policy and the work of public administrators implementing those policies were much better for some citizens than for others. Issues of racial and class inequality and injustice were everywhere evident and the subject of open anger, indignation, outrage, and passion. Riots in the streets over racial injustice and an unpopular war tend to concentrate the mind. It was in this state of concentration that the phrase "social equity" entered the literature and later the practices of public administration, with an attendant set of concepts and a cluster of shared values.

In a brief and summary form, the initial elements of the concept of social equity are found in the claim that justice, fairness, and equality have everything to do with public administration. First, laws do not carry out themselves; implementation is our work. Second, if public administrators implement the law, can we not bring the law simply and precisely to life as it is written? No, we cannot. The law is seldom so clear, so precise, or so evident that it can uniformly be applied from case to case to case. Third, in the early years of our field, it was written that public administration should be neutral implementation of law and policy. We know that this is not strictly possible. Public administration is the law in action and involves, indeed requires, interpretation of that law and discretion in its application. Fourth, our public institutions are the setting in which our elected leaders, working in our system of democratic self-government, struggle with issues of fairness, justice, and equality. But because public administrators are responsible for carrying out the laws and policies, we too have important struggles with fairness, justice, and equality. As a nation, we are not as fair, as just, or as equal, as we should be. Public administrators cannot say that these problems belong only to lawmakers.

In the early stages of the development of social equity in public administration, it was assumed that other academic fields or disciplines and other bodies of professional practice were also developing and embracing self-aware concepts of social equity. We now know that this was not the case. Only in recent years have other fields, disciplines, and bodies of professional practice stepped up to consideration of social equity.

So it could be said that, at least with respect to social equity, public administration has led the way.

In the early years of applying concepts of social equity to public administration, emphasis was on issues of race and gender in employment, democratic participation, and service delivery. Efficient and economical management of government agencies characterizes the ethics that guided much early reasoning in American public administration. The logic of those ethics allowed public administrators to assume that the effects of good management, efficiency, and economy would be evenly and fairly distributed among our citizens. Gradually, however, public administration began to acknowledge that many public programs were implemented much more efficiently and effectively for some citizens than for others. Indeed, public administrators could not logically claim to be without responsibility for some practices that resulted in obvious unfairness and injustice, so an argument emerged for social equity as an added ethic in public administration. Eventually, social equity took its place along with efficiency and economy as the third pillar of public administration. Indeed, by the late 1990s, these words were in Shafritz and Russell's standard text:

> The ethical and equitable treatment of citizens by administrators is at the forefront of concerns in public agencies. Reinforced by changing public attitudes, the reinventing government movement and civil rights laws, the new public administration has triumphed after a quarter century. Now it is unthinkable (as well as illegal), for example, to deny someone welfare benefits because of their race or a job opportunity because of their sex. Social equity today (2000) does not have to be so much fought for by young radicals as administered by managers of all ages. (436)

Over the years, the phrase "social equality" has come to encompass the many complex issues associated with fairness, justice, and equality in public administration. Shafritz and Russell list three qualities of social equity:

> First is the obligation to administer the laws they work under in a fair manner. It is hard to believe today that this first obligation was once controversial.
> The second way of interpreting obligations to advance social equity is to feel bound to proactively further the cause—to seek to hire and advance a varied workforce. The attitude requires a specific approach: It is not enough to go out and find qualified minorities. You must go out, find them, and then qualify them. This is why the U.S. armed forces have been so much more successful in their affirmative action efforts than the society as a whole.
> Third, government can go only so far in forcing social equity. But there is no limit to the amount of inspiration it can provide to encourage people to do the right, decent, and honorable thing. This encouragement has a name. It is called moral leadership. (436–37)

Over the years, both the subject of social equity and its language have changed. Equity is now more broadly defined to include not just race and gender but ethnicity, sexual preference, certain mental and physical conditions, language, and variations in economic circumstances. The words multiculturalism and diversity are now often used to suggest this broader definition of social equity.

There is little doubt that inequality in America would be worse were it not for public administrators dedicated to social equity in their practice, but there is no question that the broader context of American politics has tilted the playing field toward the privileged and away from the underprivileged, making contemporary commitment on the part of public administrators to social equity particularly difficult.

Some Examples of the Widening Social Equity Gap

The growing acceptance of social equity in public administration over the past thirty-five years has occurred during a time when the actual status of social equity in America has been in steady decline. Although we have been promoting democracy abroad and even fighting to bring it to others, democracy at home is in trouble. The recent report of the Task Force on Inequality in America of the American Political Science Association puts it this way: "Our country's ideals of equal citizenship and responsive government may be under growing threat in an era of persistent and rising inequality. Disparities of income, wealth, and access to opportunity are growing more sharply in the United States than in many other nations, and gaps between races and ethnic groups persist. Progress toward realizing American ideals of democracy may have stalled, and in some arenas reversed" (651).

At the time of the emergence of social equity in public administration, racial and gender inequality and discrimination were widespread. But in our time, "the scourge of overt discrimination against African Americans and women has been replaced by a more subtle but still potent threat—the growing concentration of the country's wealth and income in the hands of the few" (651). Rising economic inequality is accompanied by other forms of democratic privation—highly unequal voices in political affairs and government processes that are much more responsive to the privileged than to other Americans. "Disparities in participation," the task force goes on to say, "mean that the concerns of lower- or moderate-income Americans, racial and ethnic minorities, and legal immigrants are systematically less likely to be heard by government officials. In contrast, the interests and preferences of the better-off are conveyed with clarity, consistency, and forcefulness" (658). In addition to the gap between the poor and the rest of society, there is a growing gap between privileged professionals, managers, and business owners on the one hand and the middle strata of white, African American, and

Latino workers and blue-collar employees on the other. Put bluntly, despite our claimed commitment to social equity, important elements of professional public administration are part of the problem. All of the contemporary social equity research and data seem to indicate that the terrain of social equity has shifted from more-or-less exclusive concentration on the equity issues of minorities to broad consideration of how to achieve social equity in the context of growing disparity between the haves and have-nots, recognizing that minorities constitute a disproportionate percentage of the have-nots.

The APSA task force concludes their report with these words:

> The Declaration of Independence promised that all American citizens would enjoy equal political rights. Nearly every generation has returned to this promise and struggled to elevate the performance of American democracy to its high ideals. The promise of American democracy is threatened again. The threat is less overt than the barriers of law or social custom conquered by earlier generations. Today the risk is that rising economic inequality will solidify longstanding disparities in political voice and influence, and perhaps exacerbate such disparities. Our government is becoming less democratic, responsive mainly to the privileged and not a powerful instrument to correct disadvantages and look out for the majority. If disparities of participation and influence become further entrenched and if average citizens give up on democratic government—unequal citizenship could take on a life of its own, weakening American democracy for a long time to come. (662)

In the manner of political science, the APSA report calls for research on matters of social equity and for "the engagement of political science with improving American democracy through scholarship" (661). For two reasons, however, those identified with public administration, either as a field of political science or as a freestanding academic field and body of professional practice, are inclined to a less passive and more engaged approach to the problems of inequality in America. First, the argument that issues of inequality belong to politics and policy and not to public administration must be rejected. Virtually all empirical research in the field indicates that public administration is highly influential in policy making and implementation. Second, as an academic field, a body of research, and a field of professional practice, public administration has always been applied. After all, how can we run the Constitution and carry out the laws if we do not get our hands dirty? Because our work tends to be applied, it is not a surprise that public administration wrestled with issues of social equity for thirty years before our political science colleagues looked into it. It is also not a surprise that our political science colleagues have chosen to attempt to improve democracy through scholarship, a distinctly "clean hands" approach to the subject. This is good. Let political scientists and others keep their hands clean and study in minute detail exactly how unequal America has become. We need their good work. But in public administration, I insist that we engage with the problem of inequality, that we dirty our hands with inequality, that we be outraged, passionate, and determined. In short, I insist that we actually apply social equity in public administration.

Walking the Social Equity Talk

It is easy, of course, to exhort one and all to apply social equity in all aspects of public administration. But how should it be done?

First, like our environmental friends, when it comes to social equity, we should think globally and act locally. Indeed I argue that all important matters of social equity are local, in the sense of consequences. The results of national policies are all manifest locally, in our neighborhoods, our families, our cities, and our workplaces.

Many of the elements of inequality are influenced by the unique patterns of jurisdictional fragmentation in American metropolitan areas. The concentration of poor African Americans, and to a lesser extent Latinos, in low-income urban areas has had a spiraling effect on inequality as the basic elements of opportunity—access to good schools, jobs, transportation, housing, and safety—have become largely unavailable to residents of these neighborhoods. Large-scale federal government policies such as public housing, transportation, welfare reform, and educational reform have tended either to be ineffective or to exacerbate the problems of inequality. Census data now indicate that poverty is moving into the suburbs and our metropolitan areas are becoming more geographically diverse. Public administrators at the local level are increasingly in a position to either influence policies or implement already established policies in a way that ameliorates some of the effects of poverty and opens opportunities. Metropolitan migration is so pronounced that the us-versus-them patterns of an inner city and its suburbs is giving way to "us and us" patterns of similarity between inner cities and suburbs. Like-minded public administration professionals should be working together on their collective social equity issues because it is increasingly evident that few jurisdictions can claim to be isolated from the consequences of poverty and inequality.

Second, it is time for everyone in public administration to be engaged in the war of ideas. We are, as Weir (2004) explains, still citizens: "Ceding the ideological terrain to antigovernmental messages like 'the era of big government is over' is not good enough in a polity in which simple media messages are not counter-balanced by organizational politics. In fact, simple antigovernmentalism amounts to endorsing unchecked inequality. A strong, big message about how government is 'on your side' or is 'here to help you' is essential to counteract antigovernment messages" (680). Americans may be philosophical conservatives, but they are programmatic liberals, in the sense of support for rural electrification, environmental protection, Medicare, Social Security, and so forth. The problem is that simple defense of the programmatic status quo is defensive and bereft of new ideas. It is time for public administrators of all kinds to relentlessly ask the so-called second question. The first question is whether an existing or proposed public program is effective or good. The second question is more important: For whom is this program effective or good? Answer any class-warfare charge immediately with the understanding that the second question can be deferred if it can be demonstrated that a program is universally good. If that doesn't work, try this retort: "You say that I am practicing class warfare. Nonsense. I am engaged in the war of ideas, and my idea is fair and yours is not. Stop tossing around class-warfare slogans and engage me in the war of ideas." To effectively engage in the war of ideas requires knowledge, courage, and a quick wit. We public administrators have the knowledge, and most of us have a quick wit. But do we have the courage?

Third, it is important to remember that it isn't necessarily good ideas that win the war of ideas. Determination, organization, money, and persistence behind an idea are likely to win the war. Public administrators know how to organize, and we are determined and persistent. We are natural social equity warriors. We are passionate advocates for policy specialization, and we can be equally passionate advocates for fairness in implementing it. Those of us committed to social equity should pick our cause and enlist in the organizations most likely to turn the levers of policy in the direction of fairness and justice.

Fourth, when public administration is practiced at the street level, it employs a form of social equity. As Steven Maynard-Moody and Michael Musheno (2003) suggest in their book *Cops, Teachers, Counselors,* social service officers, cops on the beat, and teachers in the classroom all live in a world of scarce resources, limited time, ambiguous expectations, and conflicting rules. To manage their way through these limitations, street-level bureaucrats apply a form of public service delivery and distribution based on what the authors describe as "client worthiness," which is based on stories and master narratives that enable street-level workers to affix particular identity to their clients. The day-to-day practices of street-level public servants is all about the search for fairness, equity, and justice. "Fixing and enforcing citizen-client identities forms the premise for street-level workers' judgments," they write.

Their stories reveal how street-level decision making is complexly moral and contingent rather than narrowly rule-bound and static. Cops, teachers, and counselors first make normative judgments about offenders, kids, and clients and then apply, bend, or ignore rules and procedures to support the moral reasoning. Identity-based normative judgments determine which and how rules, procedures and policies are applied. Morality trumps legality in terms of which rules, procedures, and policies are acted on; who gets what services and who is hassled or arrested; and how rules, procedures and policies are enacted. (155)

Maynard-Moody and Musheno describe street-level bureaucrats as the coal miners of policy: they do the hard, dirty, and dangerous work of the state. Sometimes they get it all wrong, as in examples of racial profiling and police abuse. Still, most of the time and in most street-level settings, "small acts of normative improvisation by forgotten streetwise workers sustain the state; they are acts of statecraft on which the institutions of governing depend" (165). When it comes to social equity in action, supervisors, managers, and members of the Senior Executive Service could take some lessons from street-level bureaucrats.

Fifth, like it or not, senior public administrators and those of us who study public administration are part of the elite, the privileged. In much of our literature and ideology, there is a distinctly patronizing tone to social equity. A commitment to social equity obliges us to look after the interests of those who are denied opportunities or are disadvantaged regardless of their competence. At the intermediate and upper levels of public administration, we tend to avoid the uncomfortable issue of competence, although street-level workers have no illusions about it. I am partial to the blunt words of Lawrence M. Mead (2004) on this subject. In an article in *Perspectives on Politics,* he wrote:

> To recover democracy, government must assume greater competence in lower-income Americans than the elite finds comfortable. We would rather lay the burden of change on ourselves than on the less fortunate. We believe in our own abilities; we are less sure about theirs. But, unless some minimal capacities are expected of the less privileged, change becomes unimaginable, and a caste society will emerge
>
> To recover democracy, government must assume greater competence in lower-income Americans than the elite finds comfortable. We would rather lay the burden of change on ourselves than on the less fortunate. (674)

There are two interesting lessons on this subject. One is the lesson and life of Mohandas Gandhi, who insisted in collective nonviolent expression of demands for fairness on the part of the least advantaged. Another is the lesson of the Roundheads or Puritans, British citizens below the elite who asserted a belief in the individual, independent of class; insisted on egalitarian politics; and were suspicious of elites in their hierarchical polity. The founding of the United States of America was a denial of aristocracy and the triumph of Roundhead reasoning. In much of social equity, there is democratic rhetoric but aristocratic assumptions. We search still for versions of social equity that are truly from the bottom up.

Sixth, it is high time for moral indignation, for passion and anger. The moral high ground, often put passionately as Christian doctrine, has tended toward those interested in issues such as abortion, gay marriage, human cloning, stem-cell research, and euthanasia, and those mobilized in pursuit of these issues have proven to be formidable. Issues of poverty, at least from the biblical Christian perspective, are at least as central to doctrine as are these other issues. But it is far more difficult to bring indignation and passion to matters of poverty. Still, this is what needs to be done. Describing "sinful inequalities," John Dilulio writes in *Perspectives on Politics,* "Bible-believing Christians are supposed to heed the call to 'be not afraid' of any worldly challenge. . . . Inequality is a moral problem, and [if] you are convinced that it is a real problem in America today, you should not be afraid to say so—and not be afraid to recommend whatever policies or programs you believe might make a real lasting difference. . . . It is liberals, not conservatives, who have normally lacked the courage of their true convictions, some for fear of being accused of favoring 'big government' or having other thoughts out of season" (669). Persistent and grinding poverty is a profoundly moral issue, and social equity is part of a moral stance on that issue. But how shall we most effectively put the social equity of public administration in practice? In addition to applying social equity in our day-to-day public administration work, I suggest that we more broadly engage issues of racial, gender, and ethnic inequality and issues of inequality in economic opportunity, jobs, housing, transportation, and health care. I respect those who are working on social equity indicators, social equity benchmarks, and other forms of statistics, but the prospects for success of such labor seem to me to be limited. Furthermore, statistics and data lack passion and smother indignation. It does the cause of social equity little good to be able to know exactly how poor the poor are.

Instead we should turn to the media most likely to stir an interest in social equity. Think of the statistics regarding the grossly disproportionate percentage of incarcerated African Americans. We know those appalling statistics forward and backward, and it seems to make little difference. Stories, films, videos, essays, and personal descriptions of the ravages of an overly long sentence for a drug offence have the power to move people, and also to move policy makers. Stories, films, and videos of single mothers working two jobs and still falling behind hold some prospect for moving watchers and readers. There is a desperate need to dramatize social equity issues, to bring them to life. I am convinced that if the general population understood more fully the effects of discrimination and poverty on American lives, they would respond by supporting candidates committed to social equity. Through their neighborhoods, churches, and social groups, mobilized citizens who understand poverty and inequality would personally do their part to even up the economic and political playing field.

If politics is all about majority rule—and it is—then public administration should be all about seeing after the interests of minorities and the poor. It seems to me we are long past needing to defend this proposition. It is time to walk the social equity talk.

6

An Intergenerational
Social Equity Ethic

The essay upon which chapter 6 is based was written in 1993. Despite its being written more than fifteen years ago, it has a particularly contemporary ring. Although issues such as Social Security, the federal deficit and environmental degradation, are very much with us, it is the global warming issue that is the modern icon of intergenerational social equity. Rapidly growing awareness of global warming has done more than any other policy issue to make the intergenerational social equity point. Unlike many national intergenerational issues, such as Social Security or the federal deficit, global warming is genuinely international and intergovernmental. It is also both governmentally and technologically complex, thereby calling for governmental knowledge and skills and for technological competence. Which, in turn, call for dedicated problem solvers. These are job descriptions for public administrators, particularly those armed with a sense of intergenerational social equity.

Chapter 6 is a predicate for the present (2010) recession and the issues of debt associated with it. Large-scale federal borrowing to fund the so-called bailouts of investment banks, insurance companies, bad mortgages, and the domestic automobile industry as well as paying for large-scale public infrastructure projects to boost employment, is deeply intergenerational. Issues of social equity are everywhere. Should debt be used to pay high executive salaries and corporate jets when it is clear that that debt will be paid for by coming generations? Should the federal deficit be increased (and thereby increase the financial burden on coming generations) to ease the availability of corporate credit when it is generally agreed that the corporate sector is carrying too much debt? It is clear that the temporal nature of a recession trumps longer-range instincts toward intergenerational social equity.

❑

Adapted and updated from H. George Frederickson, "Can Public Officials Correctly Be Said to Have Obligations to Future Generations?" *Public Administration Review* 54, 5 (September/October 1994): 437–64. Used by permission of the American Society for Public Administration.

Consider the oath taken by citizens of the Athenian city-state:

> We will ever strive for the ideals and sacred things of the city, both alone and with many; we will unceasingly seek to quicken the sense of public duty: we will revere and obey the city's laws; we will transmit this city not only not less, but greater, better and more beautiful than it was transmitted to us.

With this oath, citizens accepted the responsibility to conduct effectively the temporal affairs of the city. They also pledged to pass the city on to the next generation in better condition than they received it. The Athenian public service ethic called for more than equality between the generations.[1] My purpose in this chapter is to consider issues of intergenerational equality and to ask the question: can public officials correctly be said to have obligations to future generations?

It seems that issues of intergenerational fairness are all around us. The current debate over the national deficit rings with charges that the debt was incurred by a profligate generation to be paid for by their children and their children's children (Aaron, Bosworth, and Burtless 1989). This debate is aside from the issue of which groups—lower, middle, or upper classes—benefited most from runaway federal borrowing. Proposed solutions turn entirely on the question of who will pay if much of the deficit is not passed on to coming generations (Kotlikoff 1992). The health care finance issue is also mostly about fairness and equity between the insured and uninsured in present generations, the old and those not yet old, the medical and pharmaceutical professions, and the insurance companies. It is claimed with considerable evidence, that unless health care costs are contained, the deficit cannot be reduced. Much of the essential thrust of the environmental movement is to preserve the earth's resources for coming generations. The Social Security system is by definition intergenerational. These are but a few of the more visible policy issues that have mostly to do with questions of fairness and equity both between groups in present generations and between present and future generations.[2]

The economic growth of the last half of the twentieth century, particularly in the United States, seemed to indicate that successive generations do better; in fact, it appears that successive generations have always done better—in the longer sweep of history, intergenerational well-being has never been linear. Changes in human conditions such as nutrition, education, employment, and housing have been cyclical (Neustadt and May 1986; Smith 1988; Schlesinger 1986; Kennedy 1993; Strauss and Howe 1991).

It is now clear that the generation born from the mid-1960s through the 1970s will likely do less well than their parents, at least in terms of comparative income. Indeed, in a recent review of social science research on generational differences, it was concluded that the next generation will do worse psychologically, socially, and economically than its parents (Whitehead 1993). Projections are that the differences between generations will widen as the baby-boom generation retires and the children born in the late 1970s and the 1980s start to enter the workforce.

There is no doubt that elected officials are now especially sensitive to intergenerational issues. This sensitivity is particularly evident in political rhetoric and symbols. Do public officials, including public administrators, in fact, have definable responsibilities to future generations?[3] If so, what are these responsibilities? Are there theories or ethics in public administration that inform our thinking about future generations? Can there be social equity between generations?

I deal with these questions first with a consideration of the philosophical and ideological perspectives on intergenerational equity, then with a presentation of the compound theory of social equity as a tool for working with intergenerational issues, and, finally, with an application of the compound theory of social equity to intergenerational questions of fairness and equity.

Future Generations as a Domain of Equity: Philosophical Perspectives

The possible domains of equality are endless. One thinks immediately of equal justice before the law, some level of equality in education, equality in voting, equal access to job opportunities, and other generally accepted domains of equality. I will not treat here as domains specific fields of public policy (environment, education, health care) or spheres of individual or group interests. This discussion is limited to a treatment of the future or future generations as a broad and generalized domain. I ask: Can future generations be regarded as a domain, or part of a domain, of equality? How is this question answered philosophically and normatively?

Classical considerations of morality and ethics often include a consideration of future generations. In Plato's "eros" (desire, striving, life as an Idea), the passion is a personal commitment to one's work, to a work that transcends the present for the uncertain future, for sacrifice not just to present others but to the remote (Hartmann 1981). The strength in the Platonic eros is the ethos of love, not just of one's neighbor, but of the one who is to be, a love that cannot be returned. Aristotle asserted that men and women unite out of a "natural striving to leave behind another that is like oneself (*Politics*, 1252 a30). Immanuel Kant's categorical imperative, as a set of principles that defines the general condition of human life, does not presuppose temporal limitations. From this ethical perspective, time is irrelevant in moral philosophy (Rawls 1971). If justice or equality are imperative principles of conduct in one place and at one time, they are imperative in another place and at another time. Edmund Burke accounts for a cross-generational community bound together by moral contracts. John Locke describes a state of nature in which we are moral equals, equally entitled to use the earth and its resources. In this condition, an individual may fairly possess land for his or her own use provided that the land is used rather than wasted and that he or she "leaves enough and as good for others" (Locke [1690] 1967, 333). David Hume, while critical of Locke's "contractarian" notions, shares his view of future generations. In his account of the virtues, we are "plac'd in a kind of middle station betwixt the past and the future" and "imagine our ancestors to be, in a manner, mounted above us, and our posterity to lie below us" (Hume [1739] 1968, 306; Baier 1981).

Certainly these philosophers regard future generations to be in some general sense deserving of intergenerational justice, equity, and fairness. They describe philosophically based domains of claims on the part of present generations toward future generations. But their considerations of morality and ethics were mostly temporal, with only very general conceptions of ethics between generations. It has been left to contemporary thinkers to fill in the details. One might wonder why considerations of intergenerational morality are much better developed in our time than they were in the past. I speculate that it has to do with the present issue of abortion, particularly in the United States, and with a wide range of contemporary environmental (natural resource depletion; endangered species; air, earth, water pollution, global warming) and technology (particularly nuclear energy and genetic engineering) issues.

In modern moral philosophy and ethics, John Rawls (1971) is the leading advocate of including future generations in the domain of justice. His is a broadly based domain of claims. Following social contract theory, Rawls develops a principle of justice as fairness, in which "each person is to have an equal right to the most extensive basic liberty compatible with a similar liberty for all" (250), and a difference principle, in which "social and economic inequalities, for example inequalities of wealth and authority, are just only if they result in compensating benefits for everyone, and in particular for the less advantaged members of society" (15–16). Choices in Rawlsian justice as fairness are made behind a veil of ignorance from which one does not know one's circumstances and cannot, therefore, make self-advantaging preferences. This part of Rawls's principle has been the dominant subject in philosophy and ethics for the past thirty years. His concept of intergenerational equity is less well known and has seldom received consideration in the ethics literature.

When the above concepts are applied to the problem of justice between generations, Rawls holds that once the difference principle is accepted,

> the appropriate expectation in applying the difference principle is that of the long-term prospects of the least favored extending over future generations. Each generation must not only preserve the gains of culture and civilization, and maintain intact those just institutions that have been established, but it must also put aside in each period of time a suitable amount of real capital accumulation. (285)

This is the "just savings principle," a capital accumulation in one generation for the next, and so forth.

The criteria for justice between generations, following Rawls, are those that would be chosen from behind the veil of ignorance and in the original position. The parties do not know to which generation they belong, whether they are relatively wealthy or poor, whether their generation is wealthy or poor, agricultural or industrialized (1971, 278). Behind this veil of ignorance, people would (should) chose the principle of justice as fairness and the difference principle to guide their moral and ethical judgments both in temporal and intergenerational circumstances. Using Rawls's words,

> We can now see that persons in different generations have duties and obligations to one another just as contemporaries do. The present generation cannot do as it pleases but is bound by the principles that would be chosen in the original position to define justice between persons at different moments in time. In addition, men have a natural duty to uphold and to further just institutions and for this the improvement of civilization up to a certain level is required. The derivation of these duties and obligations may seem at first a somewhat farfetched application of the contract doctrine. Nevertheless these requirements would be acknowledged in the original position, and so the conception of justice as fairness covers these matters without any change in its basic idea. (293)

Rawls presents the most consistent and nuanced claim for an ethic of intergenerational fairness, although it is abstract and difficult to apply.[4]

Many other contemporary theorists regard future generations as an appropriate domain for issues of equity, justice, and fairness, but they usually do so from a less demanding contractarian perspective than Rawls does. There is, for example, the argument that future generations are members of our moral community (Golding 1981). As members of the extended moral community, we have obligations at the least to do no damage to the potential interests of

future generations. We can do this better in the near term because our obligations are clearer. We are, according to Golding, probably too ignorant to plan
effectively for remote future generations. Callahan (1981) is more convinced
of our obligations. He sets out four principles that catalog our obligations to
future generations:

1. We should do nothing to jeopardize their very existence;
2. We should do nothing to jeopardize their fundamental rights to a life
   of human dignity;
3. We should do this in such a way as to minimize jeopardy to the present generation; and
4. We should use our moral commitment to our own children as the
   guide for intergenerational fairness (111–140).

A host of other modern thinkers (Jonas 1981; Goodpaster 1979; Green
1981; Hartshorne 1981; Kavka 1981; Pletcher 1981; Dalattre 1972; Baier
1981; McKerlie 1989; Partridge 1981, Warren 1981; Hardin 1980), often for
different reasons, agree that future generations are an appropriate domain
for issues of morality such as equity. Their language is often different. Some
speak of possible future persons (Baier 1981), some speak of potential persons (Warren 1981), and some speak of being and non being (Hardin 1980).
All agree that there is a legitimate domain of morality between present and
future generations.

Perhaps the most interesting arguments for intergenerational models of
ethics are less philosophical and more empirical. We have strong evidence of
a longstanding domain of allocation to future generations. Humans commonly
display a concern for the future that is part of their moral psychology (Partridge 1981). In this moral psychology, humans collectively establish moral
institutions (governments, schools, foundations) and trusts (local, state, and
national parks; animal and bird reserves; soil conservation programs; air, water,
and land pollution controls) which serve as evidence of an instinct toward
future generations. There are, Ernest Partridge argues, as many examples of
the expression of positive moral instincts toward future generations on the
part of present persons as there are examples of jeopardizing institutions or
conditions for future generations. Thomas Sieger Derr makes a similar point
in claiming that people have a kind of "moral instinct" that seems to tell them
to take some responsibility for future generations (Derr 1981). "We seem to
be intuitively aware of the wrong in imposing the bad consequences of our
acts on others without their acquiescence" (40).

James Q. Wilson (1993) reviews the research literature on child development and identifies the emergence of the moral sense in children. Two fun-

damental instincts in this moral sense are sympathy (a kind of natural caring sociability) and fairness (a concern for just treatment that transcends the maximization of individual interests), natural characteristics that are passed from generation to generation. Wilson points to recent Russian history for evidence:

> After 75 years of cruel tyranny during which every effort was made to destroy civil society to create the New Soviet Man, we learn that people kept civil society alive, if not well. The elemental building blocks of that society were not isolated individuals easily trained to embrace any doctrine or adopt any habit; they were families, friends and intimate groupings in which sentiments of sympathy, reciprocity, and fairness survived and shaped behavior. (Wilson 1993, 9)

The irony is, of course, that state-imposed temporal equality is part of the logic of communism.

The stronger empirical case is found in the simple logic of decision (or action) theory. Charles Hanshorne points out that "it takes time for decisions to have their effect [therefore] all obligations in principle concern the future. Indeed the entire rational significance of the present is in its contribution to the future good" (Hartshorne 1981, 103). If a decision, however instinctive or calculated, is the predicate of an action, then the processes of decisions and actions are always inclined toward the future. The question is, what is the extent of the future—the next minute? the next day? year? generation? or remote generations of possible people? Decision processes, by definition, cannot affect the past. We know that the cycle of decisions and actions is partly a process of informed predictions; as the future gets more distant, our predictions are less well informed and our decisions and actions are less reliable. In addition, we are not only more confident in the short-term, we are more subject to pressure to serve short-term interests (Simon 1960; Harmon and Mayer 1986; Harmon 1989).

The contemporary challenge of intergenerational fairness appears to have taken most modern social scientists and policy analysts by surprise. On one hand, contemporary social science research and policy analysis have been heavily influenced by the teleological philosophy of utilitarianism particularly associated with John Stuart Mill and Jeremy Bentham. In this tradition, decisions and actions are judged by their temporal consequences depending on the results to be maximized security, happiness, pleasure, dignity. Presumably, results can be judged on the basis of the utility of the individual, the family, the group, the neighborhood, the political jurisdiction, the nation-state, or even the world. In fact much of the logic of the utilitarian perspective is individual, manifest these days by concepts such as empowerment and choice in politics, and techniques such as mathematical modeling in analysis. This work has been determinedly temporal. As yet the tools and logic of utilitarian analysis have not been effectively applied to issues of intergenerational equity or fairness.

On the other hand, most contemporary scholarship and philosophy associated with issues of generational fairness tends to be deontological, based on fundamental principles of right or wrong. Much of this work is normative and exhortative. Only now are we beginning to see a fusion of these two approaches. Both Lawrence J. Kotlikoff's *Generational Accounting* (1992) and Henry Aaron, Barry Bosworth, and Gary T. Burtless's *Can America Afford to Grow Old?* (1989) are good examples of the wedding of deontological norms and utilitarian tools. Derek Parfit in *Reasons and Persons* (1984) builds an ethic based entirely on reason (nonreligious with no absolute moral principles) in which it is argued that in our concern for other people, including future generations, we often make mistakes based on false beliefs, particularly beliefs that individual acts can be calculated as to their particular effects. We ignore things that we do together that "impose great harm on ourselves or others. Some examples are pollution, congestion, depletion, inflation, unemployment, recession, overpopulation" (Parfit 1984, 444). To remedy this, he suggests a more impersonal ethic in which we temper our concern for our own children with a broader commitment to all children. Parfit sets out a Unified Theory that reduces the disagreement between common-sense morality (primarily moral idealism or the deontological perspective) and consequentialism (primarily utilitarian and teleological).

I return to the questions with which I began this section. Is there evidence of a domain requiring future allocations on the part of temporal public officials toward future persons? The answer is yes. Strong evidence exists, however, particularly in environmental and nutritional policy, of the failure to regard future generations as an appropriate domain. Are there reasonable or justifiable domains of future intergenerational claims? The answer again is yes. These claims trace to the earliest statements of morality and ethics. Claims for the interests of future generations on the part of modern thinkers are especially well developed.

The Compound Theory of Social Equity

To build a model for the treatment of issues of intergenerational equity, I use the concepts and theories of social equity, particularly in the fields of public administration and public policy. Issues of social equity are pervasive in every policy domain. A specific public policy may be in a general sense good but is seldom good or bad for everyone.

Thus far in this chapter the words "equity" and "social equity" have been used without definition. Equity as used here includes conceptual and philosophical treatments of fairness (Hochschield 1981), justice (Rawls 1971), and equality (Rae et al. 1981). Fairness, following the work of Jennifer L. Hochschield (1981), is taken here to mean a more equal distribution of opportunities, costs, and benefits in social and political domains. In these domains, as compared with the economic domain, Hochschield found that Americans define equity as fairness, and generally believe that our social and political domains are too often unfair (Page 1983; W.J. Wilson 1987) . Justice is taken here to mean distributive justice. Following Michael Walzer (1983), I accept a pluralist conception of justice in which there are many spheres of justice and several acceptable criteria for determining what is just. Equality is not one thing but many things; thus, equalities (Rae et al. 1981). These treatments of fairness, justice, and equality have been brought together in the compound theory of social equity (Frederickson 1990b; Rae et al. 1981) that will be used here. In the compound theory of social equity set out in chapter 3, one finds the nuanced concept of equalities rather than simpler forms or definitions of equality. In the compound theory of social equity, fairness, justice, and equality are used interchangeably. There are three primary forms of equality.

Using the compound theory of social equity, we return to the question of whether public officials correctly can be said to have responsibilities to future generations for social equity.

Intergenerational Social Equity

When applied to the question of intergenerational equity, block equalities are the most logical approach to the treatment of generations. Consider the following three blocks and their definitions:

Temporal	**Near-term future**	**Future**
Assuming four generations of twenty years each	The children, grandchildren, and in some cases, great-grandchildren of temporal generations	Those living beyond the great-grandchildren generations

Assume that each block is generally discreet and that our primary concern is with fairness or equity between the blocks rather than with issues of fairness or equity within the blocks.

The logic of intergenerational social equity based on blocks is illustrated in Table 6.1 on page 95. The horizontal axis depicts benefits, while the vertical axis depicts costs. Capital bonding for schools is the illustration.

Temporal generations both benefit and pay. Near-term future generations both benefit and pay, although the benefits to them probably exceed the costs. If the capital investment is wise, future generations will continue to benefit, being obligated for only the costs of maintenance. There are many excellent examples in both public policy and public administration implementation that conform to the logic of intergenerational social equity as illustrated in Table 6.1. Public research and development investments, particularly in health care, fit this model, as do virtually all public works investments. Environmental protection, historic preservation, and endangered species protection also fit this model. Public education, both K–12 and higher education, fit the model, particularly if one accepts the Rawlsian concept of leaving "just institutions" in place for future generations. One could argue that democratic constitutions, democratic institutions such as legislatures and laws, and judicial institutions are just institutions that were left to us by our founders and that we pass on to future generations. One could also argue national defense as a form of commitment to the maintenance of just institutions. All of these conform to the Rawlsian "just savings principle" that defines justice and equity between generations.

The single most interesting thing about the concept of intergenerational social equity is that it is so routinely and commonly practiced in policy making and public administration. The evidence appears to support the philosophical arguments of Rawls and others that just institutions constitute a form of social equity between generations and that there is a general form of the just savings principle at work. Many of the routine decisions of policy makers and the implementation of public administrators appear to support the existence of a vertical moral community in which present generations act favorably on behalf of both near-term and long-term future generations.

If there are extensive examples of block equalities between generations, what about the problems of the segmentation of policy costs and benefits in both present and future generations? Temporal equality can be segmented, as in the case of a police department deploying a disproportionate share of its resources to high crime locations at high crime times so as to attempt to make persons living in high crime areas more equal to those living in safe areas. Or temporal equity can be block, as in the case of veterans' preference for government jobs or affirmative action. Intergenerational equality may also be segmented or block in present generations as well as in future generations. Consider, for example, environmental protection as a domain of equity. The people of present generations may invest in environmental protection measures such as eliminating landfills or controlling the dumping of toxic waste. Extensive segmentation may exist among those in present generations as to who pays for these policies, depending on tax structures,

Table 6.1

Intergeneration Social Equity: Capital Bonding for Schools

		Benefits		
		Temporal generations	Near-term future generations	Future generations
Costs	Temporal Generations	Strong	Moderate	Moderate
	Near-term future generations	Moderate	Moderate	
	Future Generations			

regulatory practices, and/or incentives for business. The distribution of costs will be uneven or segmented. Some will pay more than others for environmental protection. The benefits to future generations may also be uneven, as in the case of a broadly based future environmental protection plan marred by particular locations, often associated with poverty, that cannot, at least in the short run, be cleaned up.

The longest-standing form of intergenerational equity in public administration is associated with the logic of capital budgeting. At the state and local levels of government, it is simply assumed that the costs of buildings, roads, and other forms of capital should be borne both by the present and by near-term (two or perhaps three) future generations. This is based on the logic that the benefits of capital investments will be enjoyed by approximately the same temporal generations. At the national level, large-scale debt was initially incurred to pull the country out of the Great Depression and to fight World War II, both policy decisions that presumed that the benefits of such activities would be beneficial to near-term future generations as well as temporal generations.

The logic of research and development investments, particularly as they are associated with the National Science Foundation, the National Aeronautics and Space Administration, the National Institutes of Health, and the Departments of Energy and Defense, assumes temporal investments to benefit future generations. It also assumes temporal investments to benefit temporal generations often in a very segmented and uneven pork barrel.

Certainly R&D is the key to several intergenerational equity issues. Consider the case of oil, a nonrenewable resource. If it is used up by some future generation, as it is likely to be, have subsequent generations been deprived of their rights to oil? How many generations into the future are allowed to have such rights? "Obviously if we push the generations into the unlimited future and divide the oil deposits by the number of people, we each end up with the right to a gallon or a quart or a teaspoon or a thimble full" (DeGeorge 1979, 161). We choose not to do that and assume, on the one hand, that we are entitled to use oil reserves if, on the other hand, we invest in the research and development required to find an affordable substitute by the time those reserves are depleted. Still, it is clear that present generations are benefiting at a possible cost to future generations and that the investment in energy R&D probably does not match the temporal benefits of oil depletion.

Intergenerational Social Inequity: Resource Depletion

Table 6.2 illustrates future generations paying for the benefits enjoyed by temporal generations. The best examples have to do with natural resources depletion and environmental degradation. Temporal generations benefit greatly by using timber, ground water, hydroelectric capacity, oil, and minerals while leaving near-term future generations and long-term future generations to pay the bills. The same can be said for environmental degradation. It is certainly the case that in the long run temporal research and development investments will compensate for the imbalance between generational costs and benefits having to do with resource depletion and environmental degradation. But no amount of R&D can re-create species that have been destroyed.

It appears that an intense preoccupation with temporal equality in the absence of a market economy, such as occurred in the industrialized Warsaw Pact nations between the 1930s and the 1980s, results in a particularly pronounced form of intergenerational social inequity in the form of environmental degradation.

Table 6.2

Intergenerational Social Inequity: Natural Resource Depletion

		Benefits		
		Temporal generations	Near-term future generations	Future generations
Costs	Temporal generations			
	Near-term future generations	Moderate		
	Future generations	Strong	Moderate	

Backloaded Intergenerational Equity

Table 6.3 illustrates backloaded intergenerational social equity, the best example of which is seen in the operations of the American Social Security system. While there are investments in the Social Security system by retired persons receiving benefits, those investments on average are much less than benefits received. Therefore temporal working generations pay dispropor-tionately for the retirement benefits of temporal retired generations. This is, of course, on the premise that when temporal generations retire they too will be supported by their working children.

The most interesting feature of Social Security as an illustration of back-loaded intergenerational social equity is the interaction of the competing concepts of segmented versus block equality. Retired persons receiving Social Security are regarded as a block, all eligible for benefits. Although there is some segmentation based on contributions and other factors, benefit recipients are thought of as a block. The current entitlement debate runs on the question of so-called means testing; that is, whether better-off benefit recipients, say those with total retirement incomes of over $50,000, should be a segment that receives lower benefits than the low-income retired.

This is an interesting twist on the question of intergenerational equity. In ordinary intergenerational social equity, temporal generations must act on behalf of future generations, ordinarily as a block, because the latter cannot speak for themselves. In backloaded intergenerational social equity, the most senior persons among temporal generations turn out to be powerful voices in their own behalf. The irony in the debate over Social Security entitlements is that from the beginning of the system, better-off working persons paid proportionately less to support their retired generation(s) than did the less-

Table 6.3

Backloaded Intergenerational Social Equity: Social Security Entitlement

		Benefits		
		Temporal generations	Near-term future generations	Future generations
Costs	Temporal generations	Moderate		
	Near-term future generations	Strong		
	Future generations			

well-off of their working generation (Aaron, Bosworth and Burness, 1989; Kennedy 1993; Kotlikoff 1992).

Conclusion

Should the moral and ethical responsibility of public officials be extended to future generations, to potential or possible persons, to the remote? The answer is a cautious yes. The reasons are of two types, moral and applied or practical.

In both philosophy and in the practical affairs of people, there is a pervasive concern for fairness, justice, and equity. No moral community can exist without some agreed-upon arrangements for fairness, justice, or equity. These arrangements, most often manifest in government, may appear to be mostly temporal and horizontal. In fact, from the earliest practices of government, the arrangements that sustained the moral order were also intergenerational and vertical. If, in the moral order and the arrangements that sustain it, some level of fairness and equity is insisted upon, that insistence, particularly in the long run, is most probably as vertical as it is horizontal. Many examples of temporal policy makers and public administrators acting on obligations toward future generations have been illustrated here.

The instincts and intuitions of the citizens of the Greek city-state toward their fellow citizens and toward their posterity are probably the moral norm. That we often fall short of that norm, both temporally and in our attitude toward future generations, does not invalidate it. There have been transcendent moments of temporal fairness and equity as well as ringing examples of intergenerational social inequity. Consider the great American public school system as a remarkable institution designed to foster learning and to facilitate temporal social justice and pass the culture from generation to generation. Consider the institution of slavery as a huge lapse in morality and the abolition of slavery as a courageous attempt to redress that evil. Consider as well contemporary programs for sustainable development and ecological balance as attempts to ensure for future generations the resources of the earth. Consider also the extreme northern-southern hemisphere inequities in temporal affairs (Chase-Dunn 1989; Strange 1988). The moral community is, then, both present and future, or as Baier puts it, a "cross-generational moral community" (1981, 178).

This brings us to the point of seeking overarching moral or ethical principles to inform our public responsibilities to future generations. How shall we represent the future in the present? How can we tap the human instincts toward a moral community extended through time?

Following the logic of the compound theory of social equity, public officials should seek to adopt and implement policies that support intergenerational social equity, as illustrated in the cost-benefit matrix in Table 6.1. Short of that, they should adopt policies that are likely to have a neutral effect on future generations. They should not adopt policies that support intergenerational social inequity as illustrated in the cost-benefit matrix in Table 6.2.

We recognize that we are ignorant of the distant future and we can only imagine a little ahead. Still, we must act on what we know even at the risk of mistakes. Public policy and administration is a world of creative problem solving. In the policy process, experts and specialists often define the problems and set the agendas. If problems are defined as both temporal and intergenerational, then creativity will have to find policies that serve, at least to some extent, both ends. We are more knowledgeable now of the likely effects of toxic waste, pesticide overuse, overgrazing, strip-mining, ground water depletion, ozone depletion, and a host of other ecological problems. The informed and nonexaggerated articulation of the likely effects of these problems on future generations can have a powerful influence on policy.

Many intergenerational ecological problems are only marginally related to present national boundaries. The World Commission on Environment and Development (1987), building on country-based studies and programs, is working toward some regional programs and solutions, particularly in sustainable development. Garrett Hardin (1980) and others have described the problem of population growth and the limited carrying capacity of the earth. Large-scale regional programs of education and access to birth control technology are imperative. Technology, often the source of environmental problems, is also the source of many solutions. We know about miracle rice and the reduction of famine in Asia and the Indian subcontinent. We know about antibiotics. Many of our longer-range problems, such as population control, may be profoundly ameliorated by technology. We now more clearly understand the limits of resources and the unlikely capacity of the earth in the long run to sustain a high-consumption definition of quality of life. Lasch (1990) and others suggest a return to definitions of well-being, moral worth, and happiness that are not linked to an acquisitive concept of success. The global village enables public officials to think of their jurisdictions and other jurisdictions as laboratories for experimenting with and testing creative solutions to temporal and intergenerational social equity challenges. Once a solution is found in one setting, it may be suited to a similar setting in a diffusion of innovation.

We know these things and many others. As public officials we hold some responsibility for social equity between generations; we must act as best we can based on what we know. What are the appropriate tools? One argument is that most distributional issues that affect future generations are the result of private market transactions. In these transactions, the interests of future generations are steeply discounted (Arrow 1983). The lack of intergenerational social equity is an example of private market failure. Government and public policy, it is argued, must intervene in the private market to regulate in favor of future generations. The problem is that government's attempts to either regulate the market or act directly in the interests of future generations have sometimes resulted in nonmarket failures such as Defense Department–generated nuclear waste (Hardin 1980). Still, we act based on what we know, using, albeit in a clumsy way, the market and nonmarket tools at hand. Whatever the weaknesses of market and nonmarket approaches, it is a considerable improvement in the prospects of future generations when their interests are explicitly considered an obligation on the part of public officials.

Notes

1. It is important, however, to remember that temporal equality was not practiced in the Greek city-state. Women were not citizens; the Greeks kept slaves.

2. Note especially the recent organization of an interest group called Lead . . . or Leave. Put together by persons in their twenties, Lead . . . or Leave states that "the deficit is our Vietnam." Jon Loway, one of the founders, states: "The nation went on a vast spending spree that didn't produce anything but bills. Now we not only have a financial deficit, but a social deficit, an environmental deficit, an infrastructure deficit. We're selling out the American dream. Whether you're a liberal and want a new War on Poverty, or you're a conservative and want a capital gains tax cut, you can't do any of it." *New York Times*, Section IV, p. 3, col. I (March 14, 1993).

3. The phrase "public officials" is taken here to mean elected, politically appointed, and merit-based civil servants. The politics-administration dichotomy is rejected (Waldo 1948), and the practices of public administration are understood to legitimately include policy preferences, and ethical or value preferences (Goodsell 1983). If neutrality or neutral competencies is rejected (Frederickson 1980), then it is appropriate to describe the policy and value preferences of public administrators (Rohr 1989). It is assumed that elected and politically appointed public officials are pursuing policy and value preferences. For a contrary view in which it is claimed that a nonneutral public administration will "steal the popular sovereignty," see Victor Thompson (1975).

4. Brian Barry (1978) is a sharp critic of Rawls on matters of intergenerational justice. He nevertheless supports concepts of intergenerational justice along the lines of "the overall range of opportunities open to successor generations should not be narrowed." It is asymmetric to attempt to make "successor generations better off, which is nice thing to do but is not required by justice, and not making them worse off, which is required by justice" (243–44).

7

Social Equity, Law, and Research

Putting law with social equity research may seem an odd combination. The logic for putting them together traces to the specificity of both law and analysis. Issues of fairness and equity tend to be specific to particular fields of public policy, issues of fairness and equity in public education, for example, being rather different than issues of fairness and equity in employment, housing, or taxation. The nature of this policy field specificity is essentially the same in the application of the law to social equity and in the application of analysis and research to social equity. Given the wide range of policy fields and uniqueness and specificity of each field, it is readily evident that the application of social equity to public administration is a vast and very complex body of information and knowledge. The same could be said of applications of efficiency and economy to public administration. In a play on the political truism, "all politics is local," it could be said that "applications of law to matters of social equity are policy specific," and "applications of research and analysis to social equity are policy specific." There are social equity generalizations, of course, but they tend to the abstract and philosophical. Law and research tend to policy specificity.

Both law and research in social equity are highly dynamic, changing as public opinion changes, as policy changes, as the interests and preferences of research scholars change, and, most important, as events intervene. The legal and research aspects of social equity in public administration hold the promise of yielding influential findings on the subject.

❐

In 1968 a theory of social equity was developed and put forward as the third pillar of public administration, with the same status as economy and efficiency as a value or principle to which public administration should adhere. Considerable progress has been made in social equity in the past years. Theoretically, the works of Rawls and Rae and associates provide a language and a road map for understanding the complexity of the subject. The courts were especially supportive of principles of social equity in the later years of Chief

Justice Earl Warren and during the years of Chief Justice Warren Burger. The period marked by the leadership first of Chief Justice William Rehnquist and then Chief Justice John Roberts evidences a significant drawing back from an earlier commitment to equity. The decisions of state courts, based upon state constitutions and the common law, hold considerable promise for advancing social equity principles. Scholarly research demonstrates the belief of the American people in fairness, justice, and equality and their recognition of the complexity of the subject and their ambivalence toward competing claims for equality. Research on public administration finds that bureaucratic decision rules and the processes of policy implementation tend to favor principles of social equity.

Social Equity and the Law

Marshall Dimock made this dictum famous: "public administration is the law in action" (1980, 31). It should be no surprise, then, that some of the most significant developments in social equity have their genesis in the law and the courts." "Local, state and national legislators—and their counterparts in the executive branches—too often have ignored, abdicated or traded away their responsibilities. . . . By default, then, if for no other reason, the courts would often have the final say" (Haar and Fessler 1986, 18). The courts are the last resort for those claiming unequal treatment in either the protection of the law or the provision of service. Elected officials—both legislators and executives—are naturally inclined to the views and interests of the majority. Appointed officials—the public administrators—have until recent years been primarily concerned with efficiency and economy, although effectiveness was also an early concern, as noted by Dwight Waldo in *The Administrative State* (1949).

Employment

The most important legal influences resulting in more equitable government are in the field of employment, both public and nonpublic. The legal (not to mention administrative) questions are: who ought to be entitled to a job, what are the criteria, and how ought they to be applied?

The Civil Rights Act of 1964 as amended and the Equal Employment Act of 1972 were designed to guarantee equal access to public and private employment. This was done by a combination of block equalities (whereby persons in different racial categories could be compared, and if they were found subject to different treatment, a finding of violation of law would be made) and a means-equal opportunities logic (whereby fair measurements of talent, skill, and ability would determine who gets jobs). The landmark case was *Griggs v. Duke Power Co.* (1971), in which the U.S. Supreme Court held that job qualifications that were not relevant to a specific job and that on their face favored whites over blacks were a violation of the law. The Court clearly rejected the idea of prospect equality, but because it upheld the idea of equality by blocks or, to use the words of the law, "protected groups," a strong social equity signal was sent. Race-consciousness as an affirmative action was to be based upon equality between blacks and whites both in the work cohort and between the work cohort and the labor market—a kind of double application of equality.

John Nalbandian, in a recent review of case law on affirmative action in employment, observed that cases subsequent to *Griggs* have systematically limited "affirmative action tightly within the scope of the problem it was supposed to solve" (1989, 39). The case law has sought to limit negative effects, such as unwanted inequality befalling nonminorities as a result of these programs. *The University of California Regents v. Bakke* (1978) was the most celebrated example of judicial support for block equality to bring blacks up to an enrollment level equal to whites, while at the same time protecting a nonminority claimant who would likely have qualified for admission in the absence of a protected class.

The affirmative action laws, and the Court's interpretations of them, have had a significant effect on equalizing employment opportunities, first between minorities and nonminorities and more recently by gender (Ingraham and Rosenbloom 1989). Nalbandian predicts, however, that the values of social equity may decline in a shift toward a new balance in employment practices, giving greater emphasis to efficiency (1989, 44).

Contracting

In the 1977 Public Works Employment Act, the national government established a minority-business-enterprise 10 percent set-aside, requiring that 10 percent of all public works contracts be reserved for firms owned by minorities. The 10-percent set-aside was tested and affirmed in *Fullilove v. Klutznick* (1980). U.S. Supreme Court Justice Thurgood Marshall, for the majority, said:

> It is indisputable that Congress' articulated purpose for enacting the set-aside provision was to remedy the present effects of past racial discrimination. . . .
>
> Today, by upholding this race-conscious remedy, the Court accords Congress the authority to undertake the task of moving our society toward a state of meaningful equality of opportunity, not an abstract version of equality in

which the effects of past discrimination would be forever frozen into our social fabric.

For the minority, Potter Stewart argued:

> On its face, the minority business enterprise provision at issue in this case denies the equal protection of the law. . . . The fourteenth Amendment was adopted to ensure . . . that the law would honor no preference based on lineage.

Clearly, in this case, Marshall and Stewart use different domains and diverge on the issue of what is to be equal. To Marshall, block equality is essential, while to Stewart, individual equality is required. Finally, as to employment (in this case contracting) opportunities, Marshall prefers it to be prospect equality, while Stewart wants it to be means equality.

In a 1989 affirmation of the 10-percent set-aside provisions of the 1977 Federal Public Works Employment Act, the U.S. Supreme Court struck down a 30-percent set-aside for minority construction firms on contracts with the city of Richmond, Virginia. This was immediately regarded as a significant setback for the affirmative action programs of 33 states and over 200 munici-palities. The Richmond decision reasoned that the Fourteenth Amendment was violated by the set-aside because it denied whites equal protection of the law (*City of Richmond v. J.A. Croson Co.* 1989). No doubt the set-aside provision has enhanced social equity. It is clear, however, that the law has used inequality to achieve equality.

Government Services

In 1968 Andrew Hawkins, a black handyman living in a neighborhood called the Promised Land, an all-black section of Shaw, Mississippi, gathered sig-nificant data to show that municipal services such as paved streets, sewers, and gutters were unequally distributed. Because these services were available in the white section of Shaw Hawkins charged that he and his class were deprived of the Fourteenth Amendment guarantee of equal protection of the law. The U.S. district court disagreed, saying that such a distribution had to do with issues of "municipal administration" that were "resolved at the ballot box" (*Hawkins v. Town of Shaw* 1969). On appeal, the decision of the district court was overturned by the U.S. court of appeals, in part based on this amicus curiae brief from the Harvard-MIT Joint Center for Urban Studies:

> . . . invidious discrimination in the qualitative and quantitative rendition of basic governmental services violates an unyielding principle . . . that a

trial court may not permit a defendant local government to rebut substantial statistical evidence of discrimination on the basis of race by entering a general disclaimer of illicit motive or by a loose and undocumented plea of administrative convenience. No such defense can be accepted as an adequate rebuttal of a prima facie case established by uncontroverted statistical evidence of an overwhelming disparity in the level and kind of public services rendered to citizens who differ neither in terms of desire nor need, but only in the color of their skin. (Haar and Fessler 1986, 14)

While the appellate court ruled in Hawkins's favor, it construed the issue of equal protection so narrowly as to all but preclude significant court intervention in service allocation decisions where intent to discriminate cannot be conclusively demonstrated.

Education

Desegregation of public schools following *Brown v. Board of Education* has resulted in varied and creative ways to define and achieve equality. Busing, a means of achieving at least the appearance of block equality, has been primarily from the inner city out. Magnet schools are an attempt to equalize the racial mix via busing in the other direction. Building schools at the margins of primarily white and primarily black (or Hispanic) neighborhoods preserves the concept of the neighborhood school while achieving integration. The major problem has been jurisdictional or, to use the language of equality, domain. The familiar inner-city, primarily nonwhite school district surrounded by suburban, primarily white school districts significantly limits the possible equalizing effects of *Brown v. Board of Education*. This is especially the case when wealth and tax base follow white movement to the suburbs. State courts have in many places interpreted the equality clauses of state constitutions to bring about greater equality. Beginning with *Serrano v. Priest* in California (1978), state equalization formulas for school funding have in many states required the augmentation of funding in poor districts. Ordinarily this is done on a dollar-per-student basis. This procedure broadens the domain of the issue to the state, and it is also a simple formula for individual equality. It does, of course, bring about this equality by race-based inequality.

From the point of view of competing concepts of equality, the Kansas City Missouri School District desegregation cases may be the most interesting. After *Brown v. Board of Education* determined that separate but equal schooling was in fact unequal and unconstitutional, two questions remained. Was it sufficient for school districts and state departments of education to stop segregating? Or was it necessary to repair the damage done by a century of racially separate school systems? In *United States v. Jefferson County Board of Education* (1972) the court of appeals declared that school officials "have an affirmative duty under the Fourteenth Amendment to bring about an integrated unitary school system in which there are no Negro schools and no white schools—just schools. . . . In fulfilling this duty it is not enough for school authorities to offer Negro children the opportunity to attend formerly all-white schools. The necessity of overcoming the effects of the dual school system in this circuit requires integration of faculties, facilities and activities as well as students" (*Green v. School Board* 1968).

In *Swann v. Charlotte-Mecklenburg Board of Education* (1971), the U.S. Supreme Court stated that "the objective today remains to eliminate from the public schools all vestiges of state imposed segregation."

Two conditions pertain in Kansas City, Missouri. First is a dual housing market that came about from an interaction between private and governmental parties in the real estate industry, resulting in racially segregated residential areas that are roughly mirrored by racially segregated schools. Originally segregated all-black schools are now schools of mostly black students and teachers. The eleven suburban school districts surrounding Kansas City have almost all white students and teachers.

In *Jenkins v. State of Missouri* in 1984, the trial court under Judge Clark found the Kansas City Missouri School District and the state of Missouri liable for the unconstitutional segregation of the public schools. The problem, of course, was the remedy. It is one thing to identify inequality; it is another to achieve equality. The school district tried and failed to secure passage of tax levies and bond issues to comply with Judge Clark's order.

Following the *Liddell* case, Judge Clark ordered both tax increases and bond issuances to cover the remedies sought in 1986 (*Liddell v. State of Missouri* 1984). The court also held that 75 percent of the cost of the plan was allocated to the State of Missouri for funding. The appellate court sustained all of Judge Clark's remedies with the exception of a 1.5-percent surcharge on incomes earned in Kansas City by nonresidents and instructed the state and the district to proceed with the remedies (*State of Missouri v. Jenkins* 1995).

If the majority of the citizens had turned down bond issues and had refused higher taxation to enable the school district to meet its desegregation objectives, how could the judge justify imposing those taxes as a matter of law? He said,

> a majority has no right to deny others the constitutional guarantees to which they are entitled. This court, having found that vestiges of unconstitutional discrimination still exist in the KCMSD is not so callous as to accept the

proposition that it is helpless to enforce a remedy to correct the past viola-
tions. . . . The court must weigh the constitutional rights of the taxpayers
against the constitutional rights of the plaintiff students in this case. The
court is of the opinion that the balance is clearly in favor of the students
who are helpless without the aid of this court. (*Jenkins v. State of Missouri*
672 F. Supp. 412 1984c).

From an equality point of view, there are several examples of competing
concepts of fairness. First, with the individual definition of equality, each
vote is equal to each other vote, and the majority wins in a representative
democracy. The court here clearly said that a majority cannot vote away the
constitutional rights of a minority to equal schooling. Second is the dimen-
sion of time or intergenerational equality. The century of inequality in schools
for black children was to be remedied by a period of inequality toward nonminorities to correct for the past. Third is the question of domain. To what
extent should the issue be confined to one school district? Because schools are
constitutionally established in the state of Missouri, Judge Clark concluded
that the funding solutions for desegregation were ultimately the responsibility
of the state. Indeed, Arthur A. Bensen II, an attorney for the plaintiff, argued
persuasively that it was fully within the authority of Judge Clark not only
to impose either state- or area wide financing to solve school desegregation
but also to reorganize the school districts to eliminate the vestiges of prior
discrimination (Bensen 1985). The judge chose not to go that far. Many more
examples of equality can be traced to the courts, including equalizing funding
for male and female student athletes in schools and colleges.

An especially interesting and relevant interpretation of the relationship
between social equity and law as they have to do with public administration
is provided by Charles M. Haar and Daniel W. Fessler. They suggest that the
basis for equality in the law is less likely to be found in the U.S. Constitution and federal statutes and more likely to be found in state constitutions
and statutes. "Recognizing the growing practical difficulties in relying on
the equal protection clause, we assert the existence—the convincing and
determinative presence—of a common law doctrine, the duty to serve, as an
avenue of appeal that predates the federal Constitution" (1986, 43). More
than 700 years before the Constitution, judge-made law in the England of
Henry VIII held that, "at a fundamental level of social organization, all persons similarly situated in terms of need have an enforceable claim of equal,
adequate and nondiscriminatory access to essential services; in addition this
doctrine makes such legal access largely a governmental responsibility" (21).
All monopolies—states, districts, utilities—are in the common law "clothed
with a public interest" and obligated to the "doctrine of equal service." If

Haar and Fessler are right and if the state-based school funding equalization cases are illustrative, social equity will emerge at the grass roots rather than be imposed by the federal courts.

Social Equity and Analysis

Consequent with the development of theories of distributive justice and the law of equality has been the emergence of policy analysis. Over the past twenty-five years, many of America's major universities have established schools of public policy that specialize in the interdisciplinary study of policy issues. In addition, many existing schools and departments of public administration have started to emphasize the policy analysis perspective. Virtually every policy field—health care, transportation, law enforcement, fire protection, housing, education, natural resources and the environment, national defense—is now the subject of regular review and analysis. Generalized scholarly journals as well as journals specializing in some policy fields are now available, and virtually every issue has articles dealing with some form of equity.

Both the ideological and methodological perspectives in policy analysis have been dominated by economics. Although governments are not markets, market-model applications are widely used in policy analysis. The logic is simple. If, in economic theory, both individuals and firms maximize their utilities, their citizens and government bureaus do the same. This perspective has been especially compatible with popular contemporary governmental ideas such as deregulation, privatization, school vouchers, public-private partnerships, cut-back management, and the minimalist or so-called night watchman view of American government. While the economic model has been a powerful influence on policy analysis, it has been tempered, especially in recent years, by use of measures of both general and individual well-being that are more compatible with governmental goals. Long-standing and powerful governmental concepts, such as justice, fairness, individual rights, and equality, are now being measured and used in analysis. Broad collective measures, the so-called social indicators, such as unemployment and homelessness, are now more often used in policy analysis. Measurements of variations in the distribution of public services by age, race, gender, income, and the like are relatively routine. Social equity concepts are used not only as theory or as legal standards but as measures or variables in research. The problem, of course, in social equity analysis, as in the use of social equity in law or theory, is the compound character of equality.

At the level of the individual, data and findings are now available that map, in a rudimentary way, personal views and preferences regarding equality. Jennifer Hochschield (1981) has determined that people have contradictory views of equality, which are not determined so much by income level or political ideology as by more subtle distinctions. People have varied opinions about equality depending on what domain of life is being considered and how equality is being defined. Using three different domains—social (including home, family, school, and community), economic (including jobs, wages, taxes, and wealth), and political (including voting, representation, and law)—and two conceptions of equality—first, equal shares and equal procedures, and second, differentiation (a combination of segmented equality and means-based equality of opportunity)—Hochschield's findings are as follows.

In the social domain, people hold strongly to norms of equal shares and equal procedures. Equal treatment of children, one spouse, equal sacrifice for the family, and equal treatment in the neighborhood mark the general views of the poor, the middle class, and the rich. In schools, equal or fair procedures are important to just determination of grades. Families tend to move somewhat away from strict individual equality in schools toward a differentiation based upon investment, such as the handicapped child's needing more, an example of Rawlsian justice. And there is evidence of a differentiation of investment for the more gifted or those with greater potential. People are not, however, equally happy with the egalitarian character of social life. If they feel they have some control over their fate and are able to act on the principles of equality, they are happier. If not, they are bitter and unhappy.

These same people endorse differentiation or means-based equality in the economic domain. People, in other words, want an equal chance to become unequal. Productivity should be rewarded; the poor feel this would produce more equal incomes, while the rich believe it would result in less equal incomes. Private property is deeply supported. Accumulated wealth is not generally opposed by poor or rich, and both strongly oppose inheritance taxes. And both partially abandon their different views when it comes to poverty, feeling that "something should be done."

In the political domain, these people are egalitarian again. Political and civil rights should be distributed equally to all. "They want tax and social welfare policies mainly to take from the rich and give to the poor and middle classes. Their vision of utopia always includes more equality . . ." (Hochschield 1981, 181). There is deep resentment over perceived unfairness resulting from loopholes in the graduated income tax because it treats people unequally. Many people endorse tuition subsidies for the poor, housing subsidies, and even a national health insurance.

Yet, with all of this, Hochschield found ambivalence. People recognize that their views are sometimes inconsistent or that they are confused. And there is some helplessness and anger over whom to blame for inequality or how to make things better.

As the different domains of people's lives best explain how they feel about equality, they also generally conform to the compound conception of social equity set out in Chapter 3. Both in the theoretical model and in people's outlooks, equality splits into equalities depending on domains, dimensions of time, jurisdictions, abilities, effort, and luck.

Field research on the distribution of local government service is filled with implications for social equity and public administration. Much of this research tests the "underclass hypothesis." If one accepts that hypothesis, it follows that the distribution of libraries, parks, fire protection, water, sewers, policy protection, and education services follows power, wealth, and racial variations. The findings of research on municipal services generally indicate that the underclass hypothesis does not hold (Lineberry 1977). Fixed services such as parks and libraries exhibit "unpatterned inequalities" that are not correlated with power, wealth, or race. These inequalities are more a function of the age of the neighborhood and the condition of housing. Mobile services such as police and fire protection tend to be distributed relatively equally, and such variation as can be determined is not associated with race or wealth. On the burden side, evidence indicates that property tax assessments are unequal in the direction of lower proportionate assessments for minorities and the poor and higher proportionate assessments for the rich and the white (Lineberry 1977).

Both interdistrict and intradistrict school funding variations have tended, on the other hand, to confirm the underclass hypothesis. In the past thirty years, primarily as a result of court cases, more than half of the states have undertaken school-finance reforms designed to equalize funding between schools within districts or between districts. When compared to states without school-finance reforms, the reform states now evidence greater equity in per-student funding (Stiefel and Berne 1981).

Why has the underclass hypothesis not been demonstrated in field research, except in the case of schools? Robert Lineberry and others argue persuasively that urban and state bureaucracies, following patterned decision rules or service delivery rules, have distributed public services in such a way as to ameliorate the effects of poverty and race. The effects of municipal reform, including city managers, merit-based bureaucracies, at-large elections, nonpartisan elections, and the like, have strengthened the public services at the local level. The public services are routinized, patterned, incremental, and predictable, following understood or accepted decision rules or service delivery rules. Police and fire rules require decentralization and wide discretion in deployment of staff and equipment. Social services tend to respond to stated demands. Each service has some basis for its service delivery rules (Lineberry 1977; Jones, Greenberg, Kaufman, and Drew 1978).

What is most significant here is that it is bureaucracy, professional public administration, particularly in larger cities, that distributes public services either generally equally or in the direction of those especially in need. The point is that public administration understands and practices social equity. Social equity is understood or given, in the same way as efficiency or economy, in general public administration practice.

What explains school funding inequities? School bureaucracies have virtually no control over interdistrict funding levels. What explains Shaw, Mississippi, and other glaring examples of race-based service inequity? Often it is the lack of a genuinely professional public service.

Conclusions

While the more abstract theories of distributive justice were found to be intellectually challenging, the theories that hold the most promise for both empirical verification and practical application to social equity and public administration are those that dissect the subject and illuminate the complexity of equality as an idea and a guide. That theory, coupled with the methodological tools of policy analysts, facilitates examination of the distribution of burdens and benefits so as to make informed decisions that are fair. Legally, equality issues probably reached their zenith in the latter stages of the Warren Court. The Burger, Rehnquist, and Roberts courts have narrowed the emphasis on affirmative action, equity in service distribution, and the like.

For social equity to be a standard for policy judgment and public action, analysis must move from equality to equalities and equity to equities. A compound theory of social equity that details alternative and sometimes competing forms of equality will serve to better inform the practice of public administration. It will always be the task of public servants to balance the needs for efficiency, economy, and social equity—but there can be no balance if public servants understand only the complexities of economy and efficiency but cannot plumb the details of fairness and equality.

A nascent theory is presented here. A fully developed compound theory of social equity and public administration is the theoretical and research objective. Such a theory needs to be parsed by policy field and informed by the effects of federalism. It must define, if not predict, the effects of alternative policies, organizational structures, and management styles on the equity of public programs.

It is a great irony of these times that all of this has occurred during a period referred to as the "age of the new individualism" or the "age of narcissism" (Lasch 1978). The dominant political ethos has been pro-business and antigovernment, antitax, antiwelfare, and particularly antibureaucracy. This ideological consensus seems to indicate that the majority share this ethos. Yet, under the surface of majoritarian consensus, one sees a significant adjustment of the workforce from primary production to information and service at net lower wages, a sharp increase in two-worker families, a profound discontinuity in income and ability to acquire housing, transportation, and food, an increase in homelessness, and an increase in poverty (Levy 1987). Thus, while social equity has undergone development as a theory—and while public administrators have, following a social equity ethic, ameliorated the effects of inequality—still inequality has increased as a fact (Wilson 1987).

Most important in these conclusions is the research that indicates that public administration tends to practice social equity, which is no surprise to those who are in public management at the local level. Public administrators solve problems, ameliorate inequalities, exercise judgment in service allocation matters, and use discretion in the application of generalized policy. Fairness and equity have always been common-sense guides for action. Some are concerned that this seems to put bureaucracy in a political role (Hero 1986). No doubt exists that public administration is a form of politics. The issue is, what theories and beliefs guide public administrators' actions? As it has evolved, social equity has served to order the understanding of public administration and to inform the judgment necessary to be both effective and fair.

8

When Education Quality Speaks, Education Equality Answers

Chapter 8 was written in 2008. As the reader will readily note, an application of the logic of social equity in public administration to the field of public education has the great advantage of wrestling with two of the primary forces in modern public administration. One, of course, is social equity. The other is the powerful performance measurement reform movement. In the context of the application of the No Child Left Behind performance measurement regime, and the equally compelling legal and political expectations that schooling be fair and equal, public education is a crucible of these forces.

◻

This is an essay about school accountability and performance. I shall defend the claim that the contemporary school accountability and performance movement is best understood in the context of two primary public school policy objectives: education quality and education equality. The burden of my argument is that the modern school accountability and performance movement has been pulled back and forth along a sweeping arc of history, first in the direction of education quality at one pole of the arc and then in the direction of education equality at the other pole.

American public education has always been about educational achievement, on one hand, and educational opportunity, on the other. Educational achievement has to do with student and teacher merit, quality, grades, advancement, capability, performance, and work. Educational opportunity has to do with justice, fairness, and an equal chance for students and their families. Both education quality and education equality matter importantly because our public education system is still the primary engine driving the allocation of social and economic goods, and the level of one's education is still the best predictor of one's future success or achievement.

At the policymaking level as well as at the level of policy implementation in the day-to-day operation of schools, the values of educational quality and achievement often compete with the values of fairness and equality. The public and their democratic representatives want, indeed demand, both quality and equality, as if they are noncompetitive objectives and as if seeking more of one will not be at the expense of the other. But in the recent arc of public education history, say the last thirty years, the magnetic pull of the values of school and student achievement have been much stronger than the pull of the values of equality and opportunity.

This is an argument about cycles of history and a claimed dichotomy between quality and equality in those cycles. While I will go from time to time on excursions into political, intellectual, and educational history, my main purpose is not historical. I shall attempt a light phenomenology of reform involvements and disappointments that is meant to account for the swings or the arcs of change from education quality to education equality and back again. And in this phenomenology, I shall attempt, from time to time, to fix the part that special education has played in these arcs.

The claims made here are fashioned after two similar approaches to accounting for or explaining competing forces of reform in the public sector. In separate works, Herbert Kaufman and Albert Hirschman describe the adoption of policy changes and subsequent disappointment with those changes as the essential dynamic that explains cycles of government reform (Kaufman 1991; Hirschman 1982, 1991). One version of this dynamic accounts for the American economic depression in the 1930s, the New Deal response to that depression, and then, beginning in the 1970s, a distinct swing back in the direction of deregulation, unfettered capitalism, and market solutions. Another version of this dynamic, and the one most particularly applicable to public education, is the arc of change from public institutions built on the values of efficiency, professionalism, and neutral competence, and our subsequent disappointment with them, followed by institutional changes built on the values of executive leadership. The point is that institutions are imperfect, disappointment almost always sets in, and we respond to that disappointment by reforming our institutions. This is essentially the story of the arcs of education equality reform and education quality reform.

One particularly important factor explains the arc of policy change in a field such as education. Public attention and particularly the attention of elected officials is a scarce and limited resource. A high level of public attention toward a particular public problem or persuasive reform is often at the expense of possible attention given to other problems or reforms. In organizational decision making, as Herbert Simon explained, we practice bounded rationality. One of the bounds or limitations on organizational rationality is the scarcity of attention space (Simon 1998).

On September 25, 1957, nine black children integrated Central High School in Little Rock, Arkansas. Ten days later, on October 5, 1957, the Soviet Union launched Sputnik, the world's first Earth-orbiting satellite. Triggered by the Supreme Court's *Brown v. Board of Education* case three years earlier, the integration of the Little Rock schools set off waves of education equality reforms that continued through much of the rest of the twentieth century. Sputnik set in motion waves of education quality reforms that gathered strength through the twentieth century, culminating in the No Child Left Behind (NCLB) tsunami in 2002. It could be said that both of these great modern epochs, the equality in education epoch and the quality in education epoch, began at about the same time fifty years ago.

The Arc of Education Equality Reform

Following *Brown v. Board of Education* and the Little Rock Nine, the courts in many states decided that public schooling was distinctly unequal and that such inequality was unconstitutional. The remedies—school spending equalization and busing—were put in place after bruising legal battles in the courts and political battles that pitted representatives of rural and suburban areas against representatives from inner cities. As the years went by, it became evident that equal per-pupil spending did make inner-city schools more equal to suburban schools and significantly improved the performance of inner-city schools. But equal per-pupil spending did not eliminate the performance gap between inner-city and suburban schools. Busing and other systems of school desegregation were likewise successful, at least in terms of integration. However, busing did not eliminate the performance gap between children from the inner city and children from the suburbs, even when they went to the same schools.

Gradually, equality reforms lost their momentum. In California and Texas—hotbeds of school spending equalization—and in several other states, politics moved steadily away from equality reforms, and state courts were less inclined to support such reforms. Busing was discontinued, and other forms of educational special treatment based on poverty, race, or ethnicity faced stiff opposition on the grounds that such treatment was unequal. Put another way, education equality reforms often involved spending more on poor and minority children in an effort to make them more nearly equal to more advantaged children. Unequal inputs were justified by education equality reformers so as to achieve more nearly equal education results outputs. In a profound irony, the language of inequality would come to be used as a weapon against busing and equal spending on the grounds that such programs gave more to poor and minority children. By the 1990s, the school reform emphasis had shifted from equality toward individual and school "merit."

The other key feature of modern education equality reform started at about the same time. In 1965 President Lyndon Johnson signed the Elementary and Secondary Education Act (ESEA), the first major piece of legislation that addressed inequality of students, specifically those from low-income families. The next year, 1966, the Elementary and Secondary Education Act was amended to include two parts aimed specifically at students with disabilities. First, Congress established the Bureau of Education of the Handicapped and the National Advisory Council for the Benefit of Students with Disabilities. Second, Title VI was established to help create and fund educational programs for students with disabilities, authorizing grants for states to pass along to institutions and schools that served students with disabilities. This was the first federal government legislation that required a free and appropriate education for students with disabilities.

Both pieces of legislation had an enormous impact on the educational systems of the time. By some estimates, federal spending on students in grades K–12 tripled because of ESEA. As a successful part of Johnson's war on poverty, ESEA provided specifically for children in need (minority students, low-income students, bilingual students, and students with disabilities). When this law was passed by Congress, many people criticized it and fought against its enactment. Southern Democrats were afraid of the federal government's involvement in racially segregated areas, while some Republicans were afraid that the federal government would someday claim undue authority over local education decision making. It turns out that the Republicans were right; after all, they led the charge for passage of No Child Left Behind, a law that almost everyone now agrees has made the federal government into a kind of national school board.

In 1975, as an amendment of the Elementary and Secondary Education Act, President Gerald Ford signed the Education for All Handicapped Children Act. This law was created in an effort to provide an appropriate education for the millions of children with disabilities who were not receiving a proper education.

The Individuals with Disabilities Education Act (IDEA) was passed and signed by President Clinton in 1990. It changed the name of special needs students from "handicapped children" to "children with disabilities" and established the right of qualifying students to receive special education beginning as early as three years of age. IDEA offers educational services to students with disabilities from the time they are toddlers until the time they receive stable jobs. The act has been amended several times; the last amendment was signed by President Bush in 2004. IDEA 2004 maintains the basic structure of the original act, while adding several specific requirements such as those that apply to special education teacher qualification.

As we found in the case of per-student spending equalization reforms and busing reforms, special education reforms called for more to be spent on children with disabilities than on other children in order to make them more nearly equal with regard to educational performance. These reforms, however praiseworthy, were not followed by federal money, leaving school districts with sizeable unfunded mandates.

Have the education equality reforms of the past fifty years worked? Generally, yes. But, in Hirschman's terms, we are disappointed that the racial integration of schools did not do more to equalize student performance. We are also disappointed that equalized per-student spending did not do more to equalize performance. And we are disappointed that federal special education mandates have not been better funded. Another breed of education reformers sensed these sundry disappointments and mounted a ferocious response. That response is the work of the education quality reforms of the 1990s and 2000s, the subject to which I now turn.

The Arc of Education Quality Reform

It was Ronald Reagan who accidentally invented modern education politics. While he was running for the presidency in 1979, Reagan campaigned to eliminate the U.S. Department of Education, only to discover the political usefulness of the *A Nation at Risk* report produced by his secretary of education. By the end of his second term, he had morphed into our first "education president," which is ironic because the Department of Education was a Jimmy Carter initiative.

Here is a little story of how Ronald Reagan learned to love public education. After he attempted to eliminate the Education Department, President Reagan appointed Terrell H. Bell to be his secretary of education. Terrell Bell was a wily old school superintendent who had earlier served as Dwight Eisenhower's commissioner of education. Bell was raised poor in south-central Idaho and attended the Southern Idaho College of Education, the only college he could afford. Bell started out as a teacher and bus driver and went on to distinguished careers as a principal and superintendent. He was one of that wonderful old breed of school superintendents, and I might add, city managers, who faithfully followed this creed:

first, have a passion for anonymity;
second, do not draw attention to yourself or your staff;
third, when things go wrong take the blame;
fourth, when things go well all credit goes to the school board.

After his confirmation, the new secretary of education drove a U-Haul truck to Washington, D.C. In the first two years of the Reagan administration, Bell always ranked at the bottom of indices of influence measured by Beltway media talking heads and the chattering classes, which is exactly where Reagan wanted him inasmuch as the president intended to trash the department anyway. Bell's agreement to serve as Reagan's secretary of education was popularly referred to as "captaining the Titanic."

In the meantime, Bell was quietly at work on his plan. He talked Reagan into appointing a task force to evaluate the status of American schooling; after all, how dangerous can a task force be? Reagan assumed the task force would simply put more nails into the Department of Education's coffin. Bell had other ideas. The task force was headed by David Gardner, the president of the University of California and a personal friend of Bell's. The group's report carried an ominous title: *A Nation at Risk*. Rather than calling for less federal government involvement in education, the report claimed that American schools were falling behind those in the rest of the developed world and that the federal government needed to be more involved in education. The media loved it. The chattering classes loved it. President Reagan soon discovered that talking about *A Nation at Risk* drew attention away from scandals in the departments of Defense and Interior. As he began campaigning for reelection, he also discovered that his best applause lines came when he described what the federal government was going to do to improve the schools.

There was no more discussion of eliminating the Department of Education. That crafty old school superintendent had taken Ronald Reagan to school (Bell 1988). It was the beginning of modern federal education politics, the politics that later brought us No Child Left Behind. These are the politics of education quality.

Since Reagan, successive presidents have called themselves education presidents. At the state level, all governors now fancy themselves to be education governors. And in more recent years it has even become fashionable for mayors to present themselves as education mayors, most notably the mayors of Boston, New York, Los Angeles, Chicago, and Cleveland. These developments are especially important in light of the logic associated with the traditional system of public school governance. School districts were purposely set up as jurisdictionally distinct from cities, and states and were autonomous from them. The idea was to separate school governance from traditional city and state politics. The coming of education presidents, education governors, and education mayors has, in many places, turned education politics in the direction of traditional politics. Generally speaking, this has not been good news for schools.

The lesson is that presidents, governors, and mayors know that criticism of the schools is easy and that education reform is almost always good politics. Although *A Nation at Risk* marks the starting point for modern education politics, it is almost certainly the case that Terrell Bell and Ronald Reagan were supporters of public education. *A Nation at Risk*, while implicitly critical of the public schools, was mostly a formula for federal involvement in local schools and particularly a formula for federal funding to help improve local schools.

A Nation at Risk was a solid start for what would eventually become the modern education quality reform movement, which began with a group of serious reformers who had the noble goal of improving schools. But reform movements have a way of attracting hustlers, true believers, charlatans, those with easy answers to complex questions, and seekers after rent. We see all of them in the current cast of characters in the education quality reform movement.

As noted earlier, the modern education quality movement traces to Sputnik and the role of schools in the context of competition with the Soviet Union. Over time, threats of competition with outside forces shifted from the Soviets in the 1960s and 1970s, to the Japanese and Germans in the 1980s, and now to the Chinese and the Indians. The threat of competition is essential to the logic of the many consultants, experts, and policy entrepreneurs who now make up a modern "schools are no damn good" movement. Over the past thirty years, in one form or another, this movement has savaged the public schools. No longer is criticism of the schools implicit in reform proposals. Now the rhetoric of education quality reform is explicitly critical of the schools. We are treated routinely to descriptions of failing schools, incompetent teachers, and other forms of trash talk. Given this relentless criticism, it is no wonder that contemporary polls indicate that the majority of Americans believe that the schools are ineffective. The people who respond to the same polls, however, indicate that the schools they attended or their children attended were effective. The point is that the fact that polls indicate that people believe the schools are ineffective is not evidence that they are ineffective, it is only evidence that the schools are no damn good movement has been effective.

The modus operandi of the schools are no damn good movement is the use of a universal predicate. That predicate is the schools are no damn good so we need charter schools. Or, the schools are no damn good so we need vouchers. Or, the schools are no damn good so we need the profit-making Edison Schools. Or, the schools are no damn good, so we need to pass the No Child Left Behind Law. Or, the schools are no damn good so we need performance pay for teachers. The most important justification based on the claim that the schools are no damn good is this: the schools are not accountable.

The use of the schools are no damn good as a universal predicate is ideally suited to the way homo politicus thinks and the way politics works. Like a heat-seeking missile, homo politicus will find what is wrong with schools, exaggerate what is wrong with schools, and embellish what is wrong with schools. Having established that the schools are terrible, homo politicus will then cry, "Elect me, for I will fix the schools." Homo politicus learned long ago that there is no political advantage to defending the status quo and that an "Elect me I will keep things the way they are" platform doesn't work well in American politics.

While this may be very good education politics, it has, in my opinion, been mostly bad policy, policy harmful to American public education. In the first place, the vast majority of schools are demonstrably good, and, as the polls indicate, Americans generally feel that the schools with which they are familiar are good. There are, of course, troubled schools and bad schools. The evidence indicates, however, that factors of inequality account for or explain troubled schools, bad schools, and schools with low educational quality. In the language of regression analytics: education inequality explains or predicts education quality, but education quality does not explain or predict education inequality. If this is true, and I believe the evidence shows it is, the key to improving education quality is to work on education inequality.

In the second place, public schooling is an enormously complex undertaking. Our predecessors understood this and wisely devised a system of public democratic accountability that separated school affairs from city and state politics. They knew that all schooling is local and is best governed locally. And they knew that the schools would be best governed by a corporate model in which the policymaking bodies, the school boards, appointed professional superintendents to manage the schools. They knew that the checks and balances model of city, state, and national government was ill suited to the governance of schools. They knew the importance of educational professionalism and set up teachers colleges to provide a steady stream of qualified teachers, principals, and superintendents. Based on this collective knowledge, the American public schools became the great engine of social integration, social mobility, and economic development. Failing to recognize the importance of how and why American public education governance was designed to be structurally autonomous and corporate in nature, the education quality reformers have pushed school governance steadily in the direction of ordinary city, state, and federal politics. As a consequence, the politics of education has become more polemic, more divisive, and much more noisy. Why do the education quality reformers push education politics away from the school districts and toward mayors, governors, presidents, and elected bodies at all those levels? Mostly because school boards would not buy the untested reforms being sold by education quality reformers. And teacher's unions did not buy them either. School boards and teachers' unions know easy answers to complex problems when they hear them. Not being able to sell their sundry solutions, the education quality reformers gravitated into the schools are no damn good movement and took their proposed solutions to the state and federal levels of politics.

In the third place, as American public schooling evolved, there were serious design mistakes. The first and most important was racial segregation. The second mistake, closely connected to the first, was the setting of school district boundaries in such a way as to enable separation by race and social class. What was initially a policy of racial segregation is now an equally pernicious pattern of racial segregation based on housing demographics and school district boundaries. There has been no political will at either the local or the state level to fix the boundaries problem. Instead the courts have imposed fixes that leave the boundaries in place and require per-pupil spending equalization and/or busing. While these fixes have helped, the momentum for these and other education equality reforms has steadily diminished.

In the fourth place, and finally, the application of local, state, and federal politics is evidence for Kaufman's claim regarding the cycle of public sector reform. The twentieth-century model of school governance was based on nonpartisan professional competence and bureaucratic efficiency. Late twentieth-century and early twenty-first-century models of education reform are pushing school governance toward elected executive leadership—presidents, governors, mayors—and toward traditional forms of elected democratic representation—the U.S. Congress and state legislators—exactly as Kaufman predicted. This has greatly politicized school governance and seldom in ways that have helped to improve the schools. There are those, of course, who point out that school governance has always been political. They are right, but it was differently political, a kind of education politics. The new model is not so much education politics as it is ordinary politics applied to education.

For purposes of simplicity and generalization, I have used the phrase "education quality reforms." In fact, many kinds of reforms are lumped together as education quality reforms. One primary distinction between kinds of education quality reform is essential. One group of reforms actually involves some form of schooling, reforms such as charter schools, school vouchers, internet-based virtual schools, home schooling, performance pay for teachers, and for-profit education contractors such as the Edison Schools. However one views these reform models, it is evident that they are really forms of education. These reforms involve actually getting one's hands dirty in the day-to-day work of schooling.

The other group of education quality reformers does not bother to actually engage in schooling but presumes to reform education nevertheless. These people could be said to engage in the pursuit of education quality reform by spreadsheet. It is almost certainly the case that reform by spreadsheet is the most powerful and visible set of tools in the contemporary education quality reform arsenal. It has these profound advantages: It does not require reformers to actually know anything about education and schooling. It does not require reformers to actually engage in schooling. It does not require reformers to take responsibility for schooling. It does not require reformers to take responsibility for either the intended or unintended consequences of the application of its reform protocols.

If education reform by spreadsheet does not require knowledge or responsibility for schooling, what does it require? The evidence indicates that education reform by spreadsheet is antiseptic, which is to say that one can practice it without actually getting one's hands dirty. The spreadsheet reformer can truly say, "Look, Ma, no hands." Evidence indicates that through the use of spreadsheets, complex educational questions and the mysteries of individual learning and maturation can be reduced to test scores, targets, grades, comparisons, and other forms of "metrics." The spreadsheet yields numbers, ranks, and "evidence" that greatly impress the media, giving them stories that shock and titillate while not requiring any knowledge of education or any actual fieldwork on the subject. The language of spreadsheet reform is ideally suited to media coverage, filled as it is with phrases like "failing schools," "incompetent teachers," and "targets missed." Spreadsheet reform is ideally suited to "naming, shaming, and blaming" the schools. It is the natural home of the educational cynic, the hit-and-run politician, and all of those hustlers and entrepreneurs who use the schools are no damn good universal predicate as the justification for their preferred reform scheme.

Spreadsheet reform is an educational application of parts of the logic of the so-called new public management, sometimes called managerialism. The secret to organizational success in the new public management is to steer rather than row. In the language of new public management, agents do the rowing and principals do the steering. Principals set out the terms of work to be done and use metrics or measures of performance to steer agents, who do the actual work of government (Considine and Painter 1997). This is not management in the old-fashioned sense in which school superintendents and building principals managed the schools. This is the new management by oversight and accountability, therefore the use of tests, performance metrics, and spreadsheets is essential to its logic.

All by themselves, tests, performance metrics, and spreadsheets, when they are used in education, can be useful for diagnostic and heuristic purposes. The problem is steering. Most applications of spreadsheet reform in public education include targets and, in many cases, ridiculously high targets. Such targets may work politically, but they are considered by those who are actually engaged in education to be absurd. Furthermore, most applications of spreadsheet reform in public education have built-in consequences for missing targets, consequences that tend to use highly charged words such as "failed schools" or "schools receiving an F." Many spreadsheet reforms include threats of sanctions such as probation or closure.

Summing-Up: Recalibrating the Arc of Education Equality and Education Quality Reform

In the last thirty years, and especially in the last ten years, the forces associated with education quality seem to have been stronger and more effective than the forces associated with education equality. Still, in case after case, as schools implement education quality reforms and particularly No Child Left Behind, they are met with the question of fairness—in other words, education quality for whom? In each American metropolitan area, the interplay between school quality and equality reforms is played out in the context of our unique jurisdictional arrangements for public education—poor racial minorities concentrated in inner-city school districts, surrounded by better-off and whiter suburban school districts. The results of the application of the universal testing regimes required by NCLB have yielded one nearly universal conclusion—inner-city schools are not as good as suburban schools. We knew that all along, of course, but now we know exactly how much worse inner-city schools are. Now, with the authority of performance measures, we can label them "failing schools," and we can point out to the third graders in those schools that when they and their teachers were held accountable, they didn't measure up.

The paradox is this: while it purports to tell us about school quality, No Child Left Behind actually tells us more about school equality, and particularly inequality, than it tells us about school quality.

The education quality reform movement is now entering the period of disappointment, as Albert Hirschman puts it. The latest national tests under NCLB show that academic gains since 2003 have been modest, less even than those posted in the years before NCLB. In eighth-grade reading there have been no gains since 1998.

There is disappointment that the main goals of NCLB—that all children be proficient in reading and mathematics by 2014—are simply unattainable, a great example of promising far too much. The testing regimes imposed by NCLB have resulted in widespread gaming of the testing system and teaching to the test, as any serious student of reform movements would have predicted. Again, another disappointment. The sanctions built into NCLB are turning out to be both toothless and absurd. Only 1 percent of those eligible to transfer to other schools because they are in "failing schools" have chosen to do so. Only 20 percent of those eligible for extra tutoring have received it. Another disappointment.

Good politics, as every serious student of public administration knows, is not necessarily good policy, and the politics of modern education reform is a

painful example. Central to the logic of the modern politics of education quality reform is the setting of targets and goals, as if to say that schools will be
made better because a law has been passed or an executive order signed. For
example, under NCLB all schools were to have a "highly qualified" teacher in
every classroom by 2005–6, and they are to bring all children to "proficiency"
in math and reading by 2013–14. Which schools will come closest to hitting
these targets? You guessed it: suburban schools.

In our federal system, each level of government should do what it does
best. The federal government is good at collecting and distributing information
and money. We know that federal resources make a difference when they are
made available to help with education equality initiatives such as Head Start,
school breakfast and lunch programs, and special education programs. State
governments are also good at financial redistribution, the most important factor
in working around the unfortunate rigidity of boundaries between inner-city
and suburban school districts. School districts are best at organizing, staffing,
and operating flexible and pragmatic schools. It is time for the experiment
with top-down federal involvement with school districts in the form of the
No Child Left Behind law to slip gradually into our political history.

Larry Cuban and David Tyack, in their book *Tinkering Toward Utopia: A
Century of Public School Reform*, have it right. "The concepts of progress
and decline that have dominated discourse about educational reform distort
the actual development of the educational enterprise over time. The ahistori-
cal nature of most current reform arguments results in both magnification of
present defects in relation to the past and an understatement of the difficulty
of changing the system. Policy talk about the schools has moved in cycles of
gloomy assessments . . . and overconfident solutions, producing incoherent
guidance in actual reform practice" (1997, 8).

There is no doubt that the public schools, and particularly the inner-city
schools, have serious problems and challenges. But top-down, politically
driven, federal and state education reforms, based on high stakes testing and
imposed on local school districts, are not working for the students who are most
in need of good schools. That is because modern education reform places too
much emphasis on test-measured quality and not enough emphasis on education equality. We are, I believe, in the early stages of a recalibration of the arc
between education quality reforms and education equality reforms. In the coming years, the education equality reformers will overcome their policy attention
deficit disorder and come once again to be a strong voice for change.

If my light phenomenology of education reform has it right, then when
education quality reformers speak, they will be answered by education equality reformers. And the answer will not be that the schools are no damn good.
The answer will be that the best way to achieve education quality is to work
on education equality.

9

Social Equity in the Twenty-First Century

In Memory of Philip J. Rutledge

Because this chapter refers to Philip J. Rutledge and to his leadership in social equity in public administration, it is at once specific to equity in public policy and administration and nested in the wider world of nonpublic administration social equity. The chapter serves to illustrate how social equity is influenced by changing attitudes toward fairness and particularly toward governmental programs designed to equalize or make fairer. It captures the interplay between attitudes toward individual talent, merit, and achievement on one hand and problems of individual opportunity on the other while it specifically takes up the claim that measures of merit simply mask inherited advantage. And the chapter makes the additional claim that, over the long run, merit will always trump attempts to equalize opportunities.

◻

Among the better parts of being "senior" is that one is asked, from time to time, to sum things up. This essay is a response to an invitation to sum up the current state of social equity in American public administration. Because there have been similar invitations over the years, one might assume that there is little more to say about the subject. On the contrary, there is a very great deal more to say. The applied field of social equity is highly dynamic. So too is the theoretical literature. A summing up is next to impossible because the social equity terrain changes so often. Therefore, a discussion of the state of social equity in early 2007 will have to do.

This essay was written three days after the death of Phil Rutledge, a dear friend and fellow traveler along the roads of social equity. In view of Phil's death, the original outline for this essay was quickly scrapped and replaced with some observations and thoughts on Phil and on how he might view the present state of social equity.

Philip J. Rutledge and I were brought together by John W. Ryan. It was 1971, and John had just been appointed the president of Indiana University.

We were both active in the American Society for Public Administration (ASPA), and at an ASPA meeting, John introduced me to Phil. Phil indicated that he had read my essay on social equity in the just published *Toward a New Public Administration* (Frederickson 1971) and was eager to talk about it. The conversation we began that day continued, off and on, for thirty-five years. Phil's part of the discussion was applied, practical, rooted in the soil of American government and public administration—a search for the ways to make social equity work. My part of the conversation was abstract and conceptual—a search for ways to bring others to the social equity cause and, along the way, a search for theoretical clarity.

Although we were having a conversation about social equity, conversations were never enough for Phil. He was the social equity entrepreneur. During his ASPA presidency, he asked Dwight Waldo to include a symposium on social equity in the *Public Administration Review* (January/February 1974). During this period, ASPA was rewriting its code of ethics and Phil encouraged the drafting committee to include a social equity standard. He was the force behind the continuing environmental justice project panels at the National Academy of Public Administration (NAPA). Phil also was the driving force behind what is now the Standing Panel on Social Equity in Governance of NAPA and the series of annual NAPA social equity conferences.

Phil was more a choirmaster than a soloist. He gathered people together to make things happen. An instinctive organizer and delegator, he parceled out the work, set the deadlines, probed here, and poked there. When everything was organized and the choir was assembled, he insisted that everyone introduce themselves and tell their little story. He was luxurious with time. Our work was so important that it should take whatever time was available and more. Money was seldom involved, but dedication to a cause was always involved. We were all able to engage in the social equity cause because Phil engaged us. And he asked us to work for our cause. Although those of us who worked with Phil said this to one another in a joking way, it was true: "Phil takes it as his personal responsibility to go about the world creating work for others." Work we did, and blessed work it was.

We were often in conferences or meetings at which one of us introduced the other. Over the years this became a contest. Of my introductions of Phil, his favorite was: "And now, ladies and gentlemen, it is my pleasure to give you Phil Rutledge, the Public Administration Tsunami." My favorite of his introductions of me was: "And now, ladies and gentlemen, it is my pleasure to introduce to you the Social Equity Word Monkey, George Frederickson." These introductions may not have been very amusing to the audience, but we loved them.

In November 2006, the Board of Directors of the National Academy of

Public Administration established the George Graham Award for Distinguished Service to the Academy and agreed that Phil would be among the first to be given the Graham Award. The presentation of the award was scheduled for a Board of Directors' dinner on January 26, 2007, and Phil planned to be there with Vi. He died that morning.

Imagine with me that Providence has given us one last chance to have a conversation with Phil regarding the state of social equity. In our imagination, we are all at the dinner table with Phil on the night he is to receive the Graham Award.

The conversation turns to the recent death of the great sociologist Seymour Martin Lipset. Someone at the table tells us that Lipset is the only person to have been elected president of the American Sociological Association and the American Political Science Association. Someone else comments that Lipset was known for using a qualitative research methodology in the tradition of Max Weber; indeed, Lipset was known as the American Weber. We are reminded that in his early years Lipset was on the ideological left and as he aged he moved to the ideological right. Yes, Phil comments, reminding us that it was Lipset, more than anyone else in the past generation, who regularly documented the sharp rise in income inequality. Lipset regularly wrote about how the rich were getting better at passing on their advantages to their children. And Lipset's special interest was describing the increasing gaps in housing, health care, employment, and lifestyles between the educated and the uneducated.

That may be true, someone else comments, but the point is that while Lipset continued to be the leading scholar of inequality in America, over the years he changed. He was initially committed to the welfare state, to a social safety net, and to redistributive social policies as ways to level the social and economic playing field. In his middle and later years he changed to a rather passive noninterventionist perspective in matters of social equity.

It was Lipset, we were reminded, who argued that there are two primary competing themes that run through American history. One is individual achievement; the other is equality. And it was Lipset who reminded us that throughout American history when individual achievement competed directly with equality, achievement almost always won. The American ethos of achievement and of individual merit has reshaped the ethos of equality. When our language is decoded, as Lipset said, what is usually meant by the word equality is "fair opportunity," and what is meant by freedom usually means "opportunity."

In Lipset's concept of American exceptionalism, when we are compared with other democratic nations, Americans are more individualistic, more probusiness, more antistatist, and more meritocratic. We lead the democratic world in crime, incarceration, drug abuse, and family breakdown—all reflections of our weak social ties and our ethos of freedom and liberty. Yet we are more openly religious and more willing to politicize moral issues. And we are an increasingly heterogeneous people. It was Lipset who determined that homogenous cultures and countries are much more inclined to equalizing social policies than are heterogeneous countries such as the United States.

Then, in our imaginary conversation, Phil reminds us that Lipset dropped his support for affirmative action in the 1980s and was identified with Daniel Patrick Moynihan's concept of benign neglect. That's right, someone else says. In his comments on Lipset's death, Rakesh Khurana of Harvard University said:

> There are many sociologists who described Lipset as a "conservative" sociologist. I disagree. Lipset was neither conservative nor liberal, he was part of a tradition of pragmatists, who are skeptical of all grand, utopian theories and ideas. Like the late Edward Shils or Robert Nisbet, Lipset deeply believed in the social-ordering capacity of foundational institutions, like family, religion, and community. He was skeptical of big government as a solution of micro-level problems. A perspective that has recently been articulated by educational attainment and its links to culture. (Rakesh Khurana's Weblog)

When the subject of affirmative action enters the conversation, I ask the table if others have seen Sally Coleman Selden's excellent new piece on affirmative action in the *Public Administration Review* (2006). Sally is at the table, and because the others at the table seemed interested in learning what she had written, we turn to her.

In this article I trace the evolution in social policy from equal opportunity to affirmative as the foundation of an examination of declining support for affirmative action, Sally explains. In a way, I was attempting to account for one of Lipset's claims—that opportunity, like achievement, will trump social policies designed to achieve equality.

I found that with a few exceptions, studies indicate that minorities and women have made impressive gains in equality. But most studies also show that there are still gaps, and in some cases wide gaps, between men and women, African Americans and whites, Hispanics and whites, and other minorities and whites.

Over time public support for affirmative action has waxed and waned but almost always within a fairly narrow range. The point is that American are conflicted about affirmative action, neither support nor opposition holding a dominant position in public opinion. As might be expected, there is relatively wide variation in opinions of affirmative action based on the race of the respondent.

In the last fifteen years, the courts have narrowed the scope of state and federal affirmative action programs. Grassroots legislative action, direct ballot initiatives often led by Ward Connerly, the former Trustee of the University of California, and executive orders have also narrowed the scope of affirmative action.

The representative bureaucracy thesis is generally confirmed, which is to say that greater diversity in the public workforce has a positive influence on performance and effectiveness.

In my conclusions, I wrote that: ". . . despite the gains achieved by women and minorities since the early 1960s, the challenges of eradicating discrimination in the workplace remain. . . . [T]he educational pipeline for increasing diversity in their workforces is more robust than in the past, but the performance and graduation rates of minority students remain disappointing and require attention."

Then I jumped in with this perspective. One profoundly important public administration point is left out of contemporary considerations of affirmative action and the public service. Because of an increasing reliance on grants and contracts, the federal government as well as many state and local governments now have so-called multisector workforces. Indeed, for every one direct federal employee, there are now between seven and eight equivalent contract employees—the so-called shadow bureaucracy. We know a very great deal about the diversity of the federal workforce and next to nothing about the diversity of the shadow bureaucracy. Furthermore we have weak theoretical and normative positions that might account for the need for diversity in the contract workforce and the status of social equity in the contract workforce.

Ed Jennings is at the table, and someone asks him to tell us about his recent research on the influence of the Government Performance and Results Act (GPRA) on social equity. Ed explains that GPRA requires each federal department to develop specific goals and to annually measure their performance with respect to those goals. He wanted to find out whether the federal focus on measuring outputs, outcomes, and impacts incorporated attention to social equity concerns. Of the sixteen departments he reviewed, nine saw no need to report social equity impacts—Defense, Energy, Justice, State, Homeland Security, Interior, Treasury, Transportation, and the Environmental Protection Administration (EPA). The departments of Health and Human Services, Veterans Affairs, and Education have developed social equity performance measures. All told, only 6.1 percent of federal performance measures reflect social equity consideration.

As those of us at the table reflect on Ed's report, Phil indicated that he was surprised that the EPA is not using measures of social equity in their consideration of environmental outcomes. After all, Phil explains, EPA has funded a long-standing contract with NAPA to develop its environmental justice program. Then Phil says that the next stage of the NAPA contract with EPA should be the development of EPA social equity performance measures. Toward that end, Phil begins to give particular assignments to those of us at the table.

Ed adds that certain agencies that have among their purpose addressing the needs of the disadvantaged have developed good social equity performance measures. In addition, when social equity requirements are written into law, as in the case of education, social equity performance measure reporting is extensive. But cross-cutting laws and regulations that require attention to social equity in agency behavior, as is required by civil rights laws, do little to stimulate attention to the measurement of performance. On a positive note, Ed makes the point that GPRA-based performance measures provide a potentially useful vehicle for making points about social equity. The trick will be to make federal performance measures reflect social equity purposes. Phil agrees and reminds us of the big job ahead.

Another voice asks the table what we all think about Walter Benn Michaels's new book *The Trouble with Diversity: How We Learned to Love Identity and Ignore Inequality*. The ensuing silence serves as a predicate to a difficult discussion of a complex and troubling argument. Advocates of social equity in public administration are accustomed to challenges to affirmative action and diversity, but not ordinarily from so-called liberals. That's what makes Michaels's argument so challenging. He argues that inequality in all its forms—income, housing, schooling, health care, transportation—must be at the center of all claims of fairness and justice. Diversity, he argues, is a consolation prize, a second-order issue that distracts policymakers and public administrators from the central issue—inequality.

It is no wonder, Michaels claims, that diversity is a powerful tool of self-legitimization for the rich. "A society free not only of racism but of sexism and of heterosexism is a neoliberal utopia where all the irrelevant grounds for inequality (your identity) have been eliminated and whatever inequalities are left is therefore legitimated." Michaels reminds us that despite years of affirmative action and diversity, only 3 percent of the students at selective universities are from the bottom socioeconomic quartile. Universities are, according to Michaels, serving the extra-educational function of laundering privileges into qualifications.

According to Michaels, it is the ideology of diversity that demands examination. Diversity, he claims, plays an ideological trick that goes this way: "It treats economic differences along the lines of racial and sexual differences, thus identifying the problem not as the economic differences but as racial or gender prejudice." As long as no one wishes ill to the poor and the poor are not made to feel inferior, there are no grounds for complaint and no basis for challenging those aspects of capitalism that further inequality. Diversity, therefore, keeps those interested in social equity barking up the wrong tree.

The right tree for us to bark up, according to Michaels, is poverty, and particularly the structural factors that sustain poverty.

Someone at the table says that Michaels's argument reminds her of the battle over admissions policy on the campuses of the University of California. After the statewide referendum that struck down race- and gender-based affirmative action in admissions, university officials attempted to design an admissions model based on the socioeconomic status of applicants. That didn't fly. Now, based almost entirely on grades, test scores, and school quality indicators, more than half of the undergraduates on the campuses of the University of California are Asian, and Hispanics and African Americans each make up less than 3 percent of enrolled students.

What do we conclude from that? Phil asked.

Someone replies, it appears that when it comes to University of California admissions, both identity-based affirmative action preference criteria and poverty-based preferences have been trumped by so-called objective or color-blind measures of merit—grades, test scores, and school quality. So, at least at the University of California, Lipset had it right—achievement has trumped equality. And Michaels's hope of structural means by which economic criteria influence admissions policy is nowhere in sight. The poor still go to California's community colleges.

What about the Texas case? Phil asked.

Well, she replies, the Texas policy of admitting to the University of Texas the top 10 percent of each high school's graduates does appear to be more effective from a social equity standpoint than the California model. Because of the rather wide variation in the funding of Texas schools and the equally wide variation in the socioeconomic circumstances of students by school, the results of the Texas model lean in the direction of admitting more students of color and students from lower socioeconomic classes than is the case in California. But it also means that some students admitted under this policy have test scores appreciably lower than the norm for standard University of Texas admissions.

Phil then asks a more probing question about the Michaels's thesis. Virtually all the institutionalists are of the opinion that race and ethnicity have been and continue to be defining aspects of the American experience: race and ethnicity are tightly coupled with poverty. How, in view of that, can Michaels seriously argue that race- and gender-based diversity are distracting us from issues of social and economic equality? It is often race and ethnicity that put the face on poverty and give it identity. It seems to me that there is an otherworldly quality to Michaels's claims.

Yes, someone at the table says. Both abstract "diversity" and abstract "inequality" and the stylized arguments about them will almost always give way to what they have in common. Abstract ideologies are seldom fully embraced by Americans, and that is the case with diversity and inequality. In application, against the messy realities of complex politics and administration, both diversity and inequality can be surprisingly pragmatic. When affirmative action and diversity are "disappointing" we do not end them, we mend them. When the gaps between the haves and the have-nots are wide, as they are now, we work to narrow them. Diversity and inequality policy battles are untidy and protracted struggles in on-going policy wars that never end. Policies do change, though, and the implementation of policy also changes. The battle is to influence policy and policy implementation to move in the direction of both diversity and equality.

That sounds right to me, Phil says. Both diversity and equality are honorable objectives.

We may never live in an entirely fair and just world, but there is much we can do to make it more fair and just.

By then our dinner was finished. People were leaving the other tables. We were tired.

It was time to say good-bye to our leader and our friend.

10

Conclusions

Social equity seldom stands still long enough to allow for conclusions. Therefore, rather than summarize the preceding chapters, this chapter will take the form of a commentary on several contemporary social equity issues and a consideration of how those issues apply to public administration. This is not to suggest that there are no conclusions; there are. Some are found at the end of each of the preceding chapters. And some are found in this chapter, nested in the commentary on contemporary social equity issues in public administration.

Forty years ago, when this project started, the subject was equality and inequality in public policy and administration. The phrase "social equity" was adopted to synthesize and summarize the complex issues and forces associated with equality and inequality. At the time, that phrase was in many quarters understood to be a code phrase for matters of race and color, and particularly for the inequality of African Americans in American life. African Americans are still particularly identified with social equity and the long struggle for equality in policy and in policy implementation. However, from the very early stage of social equity in public administration it was clear that the issue was compound and not simple. Equality and inequality had also to do with gender, and gender intersected with color to make the picture more complex. And poverty interacted with race and gender in even more complex patterns. Further, these patterns vary by race and ethnicity, different for Hispanics when compared to African Americans and different for Asians, Native Americans, and others. Now consider these compound multiple-dimensional matrices and how the patterns of equality and inequality play out in different fields of public policy—housing, employment, education, criminal justice, and so forth. What began as a comparatively simple argument about problems of fairness and justice in public policy and administration evolved into a more sophisticated consideration of the density and complexity of the subject.

The good news is that the quantity and quality of scholarly literature on social equity has improved dramatically in recent years. Much of this literature is theoretically sophisticated and richly empirical. Perhaps most notable is Larry M. Bartels's *Unequal Democracy: The Political Economy and the*

New Gilded Age (2008). Other very notable studies are Jacob Hacker's *The Great Risk Shift* (2006); Lawrence Jacobs and Theda Skocpol's edited book, *Inequality and American Democracy* (2005); Nolan McCarty et al.'s *Polarized America* (2008); Pablo Beremendi and Christopher Anderson's *Democracy, Inequality, and Representation* (2008); Ira Katznelson's *When Affirmative Action Was White: An Untold Story of Racial Inequality in Twentieth-Century America* (2005); Benjamin I. Page and Lawrence K. Jacobs's *Class War? What Americans Really Think About Economic Inequality* (2009); and William Julius Wilson's *More than Just Race: Being Black and Poor in the Inner City* (2009). These books and others have filled in many of the blanks in the compound multidimensional matrices of social equity.

One might think that the sheer size and complexity of modern social equity applications to public policy and administration and the level of sophisticated theorizing and analytics required to work in this arena might threaten to drive out the passion and idealism of earlier and simpler work. Not so. Just the opposite. Contemporary social equity scholarship is far more empirically informed than in the past, and no less ideological. The difference is that modern social equity scholars have the facts to support their normative claims.

The many contemporary studies of social equity agree that income inequality has been rising for many years and that the gap between the well off and everyone else continues to widen. Policy matters, and policy largely explains this widening gap. The temporary abolition of the estate tax, the erosion of the minimum wage, the huge upwardly redistributive tax cuts of 2001 and 2003, are good examples of policies that have further opened the gap between the rich and the poor in America. Economic inequality is partly caused by government action. Larry Bartels puts it bluntly: "The most important single influence on the changing U.S. income distribution over the past half century [may be] the contrasting policy choices of Democratic and Republican presidents" (2008, 30). Thus, when it comes to social equity, not only does policy matter, the politics by which our leaders are chosen also matters. Since World War II, there has been lower unemployment and greater income growth in the middle class during Democratic administrations than during Republic administrations.

For social equity in public administration the implications of these findings can be a moral dilemma. Public administration understood at policy implementation is social equity in action. How shall public administrators face the implementation of a public policy that is, on its face, inequitable? What are the moral implications of the "good" administration of public policy that results in more for the rich and less for the poor? Rosemary O'Leary's very interesting recent elaboration of how public administrators handle such dilemmas, particularly her description of forms of guerilla government is helpful here

(2006). So to is Steven Maynard-Moody and Michael Musheno's in-depth analysis of how teachers, cops, and social workers handle such dilemmas at the street level (2003).

The real hope here is to emphasize the potential of public administrators as policy advisors and shapers of policy. More can be done for social equity by the public administrator preventing inequitable policy from being adopted in the first place than by the public administrator trying to ameliorate the effects of inequitable policy after it has been adopted. This requires a clear-eyed and unapologetic view of the policy role of public administrators.

The social science research literature on social equity signals a steady shift in emphasis. Concerns about race and gender have been at the core of the study of social equity for several decades. Modern social equity scholarship is shifting the central axis of scholarship distinctly in the direction of social class. Ours is an era of open criticism of business practices, contempt for executive compensation excesses, alarm at bogus accounting practices, and widespread suffering due to a global recession triggered by too much borrowing, too much production, and too little regulation. And, of course, the consequences of the recession have not been visited on us equally. The poor and unemployed have been particularly hard hit. In this setting it is little wonder that the shift of social equity studies has been in the direction of social class.

In *More than Just Race: Being Black and Poor in the Inner City* (2009), William Julius Wilson summarizes his own important research as well as the best of urban sociology. He makes a convincing case that both institutional (which is to say governmental) and systematic (which is to say routinized) impediments have kept poor blacks from escaping poverty and the ghetto. Public policy matters.

It was, after all, state-enforced racial discrimination that created the ghetto. In the early twentieth century, local governments separated the races into segregated neighborhoods by force of law. Later, whites used private agreements and violent intimidation to keep blacks out of white neighbor-hoods. Suburbanization established new and separate cities, and white flight followed, leaving poverty, poor housing, and poor schools behind. Federal highway policy provided for new roads, freeways that often served to separate the races. Until the 1960s, federal housing agencies engaged in racial red-lining, refusing to guarantee mortgages in inner-city neighborhoods; private lenders followed suit. Businesses and jobs left the city for the suburbs. Too many federally funded urban renewal programs laid waste whole sections of the city. In recent years, the new economy has resulted in most new jobs at the two poles of the wage scale: high-paying jobs for the well educated and acculturated (management, banking, accounting, consulting, information technology, and so forth) and low-paying jobs for those with little education or skills (gardening, roofing, telemarketing, cleaning-up, fast foods, and so forth). A surprising percentage of low-paying work is now being done by immigrants.

So, according to Wilson, the contemporary problems of the inner city cannot be blamed primarily on race. The legacy of racism and particularly formal public policy has systematically disadvantaged those living in the inner city. Wilson argues persuasively that public policy and the nature of the new economy have been more important factors in the persistence of ghetto poverty than the so-called dysfunctional culture of the inner city. It isn't just race, according to Wilson, it is public policy, the new economy, and the widening gap between rich and poor.

If public administrators are practicing policy guidance and the subject of social equity is shifting in the direction of social class, could it be said that we are engaged in a kind of "class warfare"? In the first place, the phrase "class warfare" is designed to be a conversation stopper, a kind of accusation that someone is taking a position unworthy of serious consideration. The accusation that one is engaged in class warfare is ordinarily followed with the claim that in a time of national crisis we should be united and that it is inappropriate for one to emphasize our differences and the things that divide us. As unelected public administrators, it is not our place to be concerned with matters of fairness and equity between the classes. Nonsense.

Consider the evidence. The two best recent studies of social and economic circumstances in the United States are Lisa A. Keister's *Wealth in America: Trends in Wealth Inequality* (2000) and Kevin Phillips's *Wealth and Democracy: A Political History of the American Rich* (2003). Both studies bring together an impressive array of information over an extended period of time, sufficient to give an informed historical perspective on the subject. Both insist on the importance of distinguishing between wealth and intergenerational wealth accumulation on one hand and annual income on the other. Regarding the contemporary accumulation of wealth, both studies find that in the whole sweep of American history there has never been greater concentration of wealth in the hands of the few. The top one percent of the population control 40 percent of the wealth, and the top 20 percent control a staggering 93 percent of American financial wealth. For the past twenty years the gap between those who have significant financial wealth and those who do not has steadily grown.

While the details are different, the gap between the annual income of the top 5 percent of Americans and the bottom 60 percent has also grown steadily. For the past thirty-five years, the after-tax net income adjusted for inflation of the bottom 80 percent of Americans has stayed essentially the same, but for the richest 6 percent it has more than tripled. Wealth and income inequality are closely correlated with race and gender; African Americans, Hispanic Americans, and working mothers are significantly over-represented among the poor. Annually the top one-fifth of Americans make eleven times more than those in the bottom fifth, by far the widest gap among the industrialized democracies.

Compared to thirty years ago, and taking inflation into account, American wage earners have smaller pensions, less health insurance coverage, much greater consumer debt, considerably less job security, longer commutes to work, and a significant jump in the percentage of two-earner families.

To return to the question: is social equity in public administration a form of class warfare? To uncover and describe inequity and unfairness is not class warfare; it is simply enlightened transparency in government and public policy. Examining social equity in public administration is a form of performance measurement. It simply asks this question: is the American economy doing well? And it asks a second question: for whom is the American economy doing well? Why should we be afraid of the answer? After all, it is actual and real variations in wealth and income between Americans that divide us. It is not descriptions of actual and real wealth and income variations that divide us. Describing variations in wealth and income is not class warfare; it is speaking truth to power. To do what one can within the constraints of law and policy to implement policy in a way that is fair and just is not class warfare; it is simply good public administration. To seek to change law or policy that is unfair or inequitable is not class warfare; it is part of our moral responsibility. To be an informed and expert voice for fairness and equity in the processes of policy formulation is not class warfare; it is part of the public administrator's job description.

From a conceptual and research perspective, this broadening of social equity as a unit of analysis and a subject for study is a positive development. It both broadens and deepens the subject and puts it in closer proximity to the full range of complex, overlapping, and interconnected characteristics of actual social equity. A compound theory of social equity was described in chapter 3, a proposed language and set of concepts designed to further both research and theory building in a complicated tangle of words and ideas. Years ago, to further systematic theory building on the subject, Douglas Rae and his associates rightly changed the language from "equality" to "equalities," recognition of the density of forms of equality, the layering and interconnections between those forms of equality, the very broad range of types of equality, and the dynamic nature of matters of equality (1981).

An interesting expression of these "equalities" can be seen in the emergence of the word "diversity" and the cluster of concepts and facts attendant to that word. At one level, diversity is a less polemic way to describe or advocate racial, gender, and other forms of equity; it is a word that is far more palatable to a broader range of people than the phrase "affirmative action." Diversity is easy to agree with and hard to argue against. Aristotle claimed that politics is rhetoric and that the quality of rhetoric associated with a particular point of view is a determinant of the likely success of that point of view in political discourse. Diversity is, following Aristotle, particularly serviceable rhetoric in the quest for social equity.

The theme of the most recent annual conference of the American Society for Public Administration was "Governance in the Midst of Diversity." At that conference, Mary Ellen Guy delivered the Donald C. Stone Lecture under the title "When Diversity Makes a Difference" (Guy 2009). She made three primary arguments:

First, diversity advances the quality of our democracy.

"The cumulative results of immigration, culture change, and an appreciation for the other, is diversity. It brings social, economic, and political engagement by women as well as men, by persons of all races, ethnicity, language, religion, and sexuality. The more we value diversity, the more we must ensure that our processes and procedures are open to all—that voices usually silent are heard; that we stand ready not just to tolerate difference but to embrace it" (5).

Second, diversity makes for more sustainable decisions.

"Gone are the days when the newcomer must emulate the usual: when women must be like men; when Blacks must be as Whites; when Latinos must be as Anglos. Decisions are more robust when they are hammered out with the consideration for, and participation of, all who are affected by the issue in question" (9).

Kenneth Meier and his colleagues (1999), using detailed school data, have consistently found that greater diversity in management results in not only more sustainable decisions but greater productivity (11).

Third, diversity does make a difference—that is why it is resisted: It changes things.

"Beware of the urge to believe in race-neutral policies (race cannot be taken into consideration in university admission, for example) that Ward Connerly advocates. Such policies require that we turn a blind-eye to the difference that race makes, or gender makes, or religion makes. Such policies are the mechanism for maintaining advantages for the dominant group. . . . Affirmative action (and I speak of it in the past tense) was nothing more than a means to override our basic proclivity to associate with, hire, and promote those who are like ourselves. Such mechanisms have fallen badly out of favor, largely because of the backlash—it perturbed the status quo and caused those who had been in the driver's seat to move over" (10).

It is notable that Mary Ellen Guy's splendid lecture was under the heading of "diversity" or was on the subject of "diversity" rather than social equity. In terms of content, however, the word "diversity" and the phrase "social equity" are essentially the same subject. There is, however, one important difference. It is very likely the case that those primarily interested in, say, gender equity, find the word "diversity" more comfortable than the phrase "social equity." The same could likely be said for those interested in sexual orientation, or age differences, or physical or emotional differences. The point is, social equity appears, in the minds of many, to still be primarily associated with African Americans and the struggle for racial equality. Much the same can be said for the phrase "affirmative action."

It is further notable that "diversity" language is rather different from "social equity" language. Diversity language is, by my reading, less shrill, more welcoming, and more openly inclusive than social equity language. But, again by my reading, the sharpness of social equity language is clearer, less fuzzy, and easier to use theoretically and empirically. Diversity may be more persuasive, whereas social equity may be clearer theoretically.

The affirmative action historian Terry H. Anderson pointed out that, "during the 1990s diversity was the winner. Democrats understood that, as a political tactic, supporting diversity was less risky than endorsing affirmative action—it redefined the issue not as preference for minorities or women but as a public good that supposedly utilized the potential of all citizens. While affirmative action drew heat, diversity drew praise, which makes it popular on campus and in business. . . . By 1996 the GOP had jumped on the bandwagon. At their convention Governor Christine Todd Whitman of New Jersey declared Republicans are the 'party of diversity,' and on ABC's Nightline the Republican speaker of the house, Newt Gingrich, boasted, 'Diversity is our strength!'" (2004, 221).

Affirmative Action in Various Policy Settings

Based on their long-standing survey and polling work, Daniel Yankelovich and his colleagues (1994) have found a pattern of consistent core American values and a range of values that tend to change. Examples of changing values would be attitudes toward the environment, sexuality, health, social conformity, pluralism, and so forth. Yankelovich and colleagues describe eleven enduring core values: freedom, equality before the law, equality of opportunity, fairness, achievement, patriotism, democracy, American exceptionalism, caring beyond the self, religion, and luck. Four of the eleven are connected in one way or another to social equity—equality before the law (justice), equality of opportunity, fairness, and achievement—subjects to which we now turn.

The policies and practices of affirmative action in the public sector have been and continue to be particularly illustrative of conflicting social equity values, forces, politics, and administration. Like many aspects of modern social equity in public administration, indeed like the introduction of social equity to the field following the original Minnowbrook Conference, contemporary affirmative action policies and practices trace to the social and political turbulence of the 1960s. Following the assassination of President John F. Kennedy, President Lyndon B. Johnson announced his vision of a "great society," and built the coalitions that passed the Civil Rights Act of 1964 and the Voting Rights Act of 1965. Less well known was the passage of the 1965 Higher Education Act, which ultimately resulted in quadrupling the number of African American students in college. Also less well known was the signing of Executive Order 10925 by President Kennedy in 1961, in which the phrase "affirmative action" was first used. The executive order required federal contractors to "take affirmative action to ensure that applicants are employed, and that employees are treated during employment, without regard to their race, creed, color, or national origin." The same language was later used in a similar executive order signed by President Johnson in 1965. These orders, coupled with the Civil Rights and Voting Rights Acts, made many forms of race and sex discrimination illegal. In addition, the origins of the Equal Employment Opportunities Commission, the agency charged with hearing and adjudicating claims of racial discrimination in employment, also trace to this period.

Policies designed to rectify past discrimination or to guarantee present-day fairness, and the administrative implementation of those policies soon came under a broad "affirmative action" umbrella, and affirmative action came to be rather closely associated with social equity as a public administration perspective. Affirmative action policies were most notable in university admissions, public school funding, government procurement and contracting criteria, and in several aspects of employment including hiring, task and shift assignments, promotions, salaries, and benefits.

As policy and as administrative practice, affirmative action was at odds with an earlier bedrock concept in public administration—merit. The entire logic of civil service rests on the notion of individual merit expressed through personal qualifications including education, experience, and the successful completion of tests. The logic of individual merit was designed to be a fair and equitable way to move away from the practices of favoritism and patronage associated with the so-called spoils system. If there is one job and ten applicants, or one potential promotion and ten applicants, or one contract and ten bids, what should be the decision rule? The classic public administration answer was merit. Affirmative action significantly altered that reasoning. If, for example, 20 percent of the population of a city is African American and

5 percent of the police force is African American, affirmative action would suggest that merit be understood to take race into consideration up to the point at which a police department "looked like the community." The same would hold for gender. In the case of contracts, a policy of so-called set-asides was developed whereby a certain percentage of contracts were set aside for "minority contractors" as a means of affirmative action.

There has been a steady decline in the influence of affirmative action in public policy and administration from its high point in the 1970s. Affirmative action was a result of the politics of the 1960s and 1970s, notably the legislative and executive politics behind the passage of the cluster of affirmative action laws described above, and judicial action starting with *Brown v. Board of Education.* The decline of affirmative action is a result in part of the politics of state level referenda and in part of a shifting judiciary.

In 1986 California voters passed Proposition 209, the California Civil Rights Initiative, effectively outlawing affirmative action in university admissions. Following the vigorous leadership of Ward Connerly, a former member of the University of California Board of Regents, an almost identical version of California's proposition was put on the referendum ballots in Florida and Michigan, where it passed easily. Within two years of passage of these referenda, the number of African Americans in the freshman classes at the campuses of the University of California, the University of Michigan, and the University of Florida declined by more than 50 percent. The percentage of Latino and Chicano students and Native American students also dropped sharply. University admissions decisions in California, Michigan, and Florida as well as in many other states, are now "color blind," based on test scores, school grades, and measures of extracurricular activities. These universities and many other prestige public universities now admit a much higher percentage of Asians (over 50 percent at Berkeley and UCLA). So, merit has trumped equity. The enrollments of the prestigious public universities of many states no longer "look like" those states. (It is worth noting here that prestigious private universities continue to apply diversity decision criteria to their incoming admissions decisions, in effect holding Asian admissions at or below a particular percentage—thought to be around 20 percent.)

Although it is a considerable generalization, the position of the courts on the matter of undergraduate, graduate, and professional school admissions is this: universities may take matters of diversity into consideration in admissions decisions, in the interest of sustaining a diverse student body, but may not use racial quotas (*Regents of the University of California v. Bakke* 1978; *Grutter v. Bollinger* 2003; *Gratz v. Bollinger* 2003).

As a result of these referenda and of court decisions, there has been a broad state-by-state diffusion of color-blind admissions policies. To attempt to retain as much diversity as possible, many states have implemented the so-called percentage model, under which prestige state universities agree to admit a fixed percentage, say 8 percent, of the graduates of every state high school. Because there are high schools in every community including predominantly minority communities, it was thought that the percentage model would yield a diverse enrollment without the use of admissions committee quotas. So far, the results have not been particularly good. The percentage model is simply a line, an arbitrary fixed point above which a potential student may be admitted. But such a line cannot weigh issues of student capacity or potential, student finances, the need for subject remediation, and all of the other factors that go into decisions made by university admissions committees. So far, the implementation of the percentage model has not significantly improved the percentage of African American, Latino, Chicano, or Native American enrollment at public universities.

If looking like America is a legitimate criterion by which to evaluate progress toward social equity, there is a notable example—public employment (Riccucci 2009). "The plethora of representative bureaucracy studies, especially those beginning with Krislov's (1974) and Rosenbloom's (1977), which provide significant baseline analyses, illustrate that white women and people of color hold government jobs at the federal, state, and local level in equal and sometimes greater proportion than their concentration in the general population (see, e.g., Guy 1992, 1993; Meier 1993; Meier and Smith 1994; Rice 2005; Wise 1990)." At least by the "looking like America" standard, social equity has been a public administration success. After long struggles, police and fire departments have been gendered and have become more racially equal. State government has likewise made significant progress, and in many of them the demographics of the state public service generally match state demographics. Following the impressive example of the American military, the makeup of the federal civil service looks like America. At all levels of government this would not have happened without the various instruments of affirmative action.

A public service that looks like America is one thing. Social equity in positions of leadership, authority, and prestige in the public services is another. Norma Riccucci points out that, ". . . conceptualizing representativeness quite differently shows that white women and people of color are segregated in the lowest-paying, lowest status jobs in government" (2009, 373). Although there has been progress over the past twenty-five years, the ranks of the federal Senior Executive Service (SES) are significantly less diverse than the federal civil service rank and file (333).

As in the arena of university admissions, social equity in matters of public employment is a venue of competing public administration values—merit versus equality. And, as in the matter of university admissions, the judiciary has taken a general position that racial and gender quotas are unconstitutional in public employment hiring and promotion. It turns out that it is easier to achieve a public employment demographic that looks like America, without using quotas, than it is to extend that demographic to the upper reaches of public service hierarchies.

Issues of merit versus equality in public service promotion are well illustrated by the New Haven case. In 2003 New Haven gave promotion examinations to 118 firefighters, 27 of them African American. None of the African Americans did well enough on the examination to qualify for the fifteen immediately available promotions. After a good bit of noisy racial politics, New Haven decided that no one would be promoted and that there would be another round of promotion examinations. The city, it was said, was concerned with the possibility that fifteen promotions without a single African American would invite a law suit claiming "disparate impact." Instead, Frank Ricci and seventeen other white New Haven firefighters who passed the examination brought suit claiming violation of equal protection of the law and the practice of "reverse discrimination" (*Ricci et al. v. DeStefano et al.* 2009). At the hearing before the U.S. Supreme Court, Chief Justice John Roberts asked, "Would it have been lawful if the city had decided to discard the results of the exam to select firemen for promotion because it selected too many black and too few white candidates?" Is there, in other words, a quota? The *Ricci* case, like many other related cases, was decided in favor of Ricci and against the city of New Haven by a narrow 5-4 majority of the court. Once again, merit, or at least merit based on testing, trumps diversity.

In the conflict between merit on one hand and gender and racial equality on the other, critics of the social equity or diversity perspective refer to the results of affirmative action in public employment as "racial spoils," a phrase that connects the premise of merit upon which the logic of the modern civil service rests with the general success of civil service in stamping out public employment based on political spoils (Will 2009). Supporters of social equity argue that there is an overriding state interest in diversity and that there is empirical evidence that a diverse workforce and diverse leadership create better working groups, better schools, and better or more effective public organizations (Meier, Wrinkle, and Polinard 1999; Page 2007). As in most cases of competing values, there are particular points or issues that can be rectified in such a way as to retain much of the value of a civil service based on merit as well as a diverse civil service. The same can be said for finding the points of reconciliation between merit and diversity in university admissions. Finding those points is the work of both practicing public administrators and public

administration scholars. Further progress in social equity in public administration is dependent upon finding these balance points, describing them and
how they work, and engaging in a diffusion, from jurisdiction to jurisdiction,
of public administration practices based on these balance points.

Before leaving the subject of merit versus social equity in the public
sector workforce, it is critical to consider, albeit briefly, this vital point. We
study and practice public administration, not government administration.
The "public" is a much larger subject than government (Frederickson 1997).
Public administration includes the work of government and all of those who
work directly for governments of all types and at all levels. But, public also
includes public utilities; the wide range of quasi-governmental organizations
(Koppell 2003); so called world governance organizations such as the World
Bank, the International Monetary Fund (Koppell, forthcoming), and many
others; and most particularly, all the nonprofit and corporate organizations that
contract with government to provide public services. The magnitude of the
so-called shadow bureaucracy is little understood and seriously under studied.
In the federal government, it is estimated that there are at least seven full-
time equivalent contract employees for every one civil servant (Light 1999).
Furthermore, the size of the federal civil service has shrunk from about three
million (nonuniformed military) in the 1970s to under two million at present.
The difference has been more than made up by the growth of the shadow
bureaucracy or so-called third party government. We must insist that what
we understand to be public administration includes all those organizations
contracting with government to do public work.

We know a very great deal about the demographics of the federal civil
service and are, therefore, able to study federal merit and equity practices.
By comparison, we know little about the demographics of the thousands of
organizations engaged in public administration through grants or contracts
with government. Such as we know about the employment practices of government contractors is based on the work of the Office of Federal Contract
Compliance Programs (OFCCP) of the U.S. Department of Labor. OFCCP
was established to implement and enforce affirmative action requirements
with federal contractors and subcontractors. Overseeing and guiding a so-
called self-regulatory system, OFCCP requires each contractor to prepare a
written Affirmative Action Program (AAP), including workforce analysis of
job titles, measures of workforce availability, and the preparation of materials on many other aspects of affirmative action regulations. A contractor's
AAP is to be based on a detailed response to the Federal Contract Compliance Manual, a guide for contractors written and maintained by OFCCP.
However, rather than asking contractors to file their AAPs with OFCCP,
they are instructed to keep them in their own files, ready in case they are

selected for a compliance review. Just over 3 percent of federal contractors are reviewed annually. While this may seem a small percentage, it is usually over 3,500 reviews annually. Regarding compliance, it is important to note that the regulations do not actually require contractor compliance. Instead, the affirmative action regulations require "good faith efforts" on the part of federal contractors to comply. Nevertheless, a contractor found to be in violation of the regulations may have its contracts terminated or suspended, or be disbarred. Such administrative actions are rare, as there are ample due process "conciliation" procedures accorded contractors by which they can achieve compliance.

Early in his second term, President Clinton asked for a full review of federal affirmative action programs. That study concluded that: ". . . the pragmatic use of affirmative action to promote equal opportunity in employment by government contractors has been and continues to be valuable, effective, and fair. The leadership provided by the federal government and its contractors has been a critical factor in causing private and public organizations to challenge and change their own personnel practices, using affirmative action as one tool to open up opportunity to qualified minorities and women who might otherwise have been left outside" (Report to the President 1995). These findings resemble the conclusions reached by J. Edward Kellough in his excellent recent book, *Understanding Affirmative Action: Politics, Discrimination, and the Search for Justice* (2006). In summing up, he writes that ". . . preferential affirmative action can be beneficial for minorities and women in a number of settings. Studies that have examined the policy in the context of private-sector contractors (with the federal government) have shown dramatically positive results" (142–43).

OFCCP expressly prohibits discrimination, on one hand, and the use of goals or quotas, on the other. "The numerical goal-setting process in affirmative action planning is used to target and measure the effectiveness of affirmative action efforts to eradicate and prevent discrimination. Numerical benchmarks are established based on the availability of qualified applicants in the job market or qualified candidates in the employer's work force. The regulations specifically prohibit quotas and preferential hiring and promotion under the guise of affirmative action numerical goals. Numerical goals do not create quotas for specific groups, nor are they designed to achieve proportional representation or equal results" (Report to the President 1995). Taken from the report on affirmative action requested by President Clinton, this quote is an excellent example of tiptoeing through the complex semantics of merit versus equity in search of the balancing points between them.

Just after he received the aforementioned report, President Clinton gave a formal address entirely dedicated to the subject. The "mend it, don't end it" phrase is often used to characterize the general thrust of President Clinton's position on affirmative action (Anderson 2004).

> When affirmative action is done right, it is flexible, it is fair, and it works. . . . Let me be clear about what affirmative action must not mean and what I won't allow it to be. It does not mean—and I don't favor—numerical quotas. It doesn't mean—and I don't favor—rejection or selection of any employee or student solely on the basis of race or gender without regard to merit. . . .
>
> Now, there are those who say . . . that even good affirmative action programs are no longer needed. . . . Last year alone, the federal government received more than 90,000 complaints of employment discrimination based on race, ethnicity or gender; less than 3 percent were for reverse discrimination. . . . Now affirmative action has not always been perfect, and affirmative action should not go on forever. . . . I am resolved that that day will come, but evidence suggests, indeed screams, that that day has not come. The job of ending discrimination in this country is not over. . . . We should reaffirm the principle of affirmative action and fix the practice. We should have a simple slogan; Mend it, but don't end it. (Quoted in Anderson 2004, 244)

The Clinton speech is a particularly good example of finding the point of balance between opposition to affirmative action on one hand and wholesale acceptance of it on the other. Although the Clinton-authorized study and report and his speech are now nearly fifteen years old, the study findings are essentially still accurate and his "mend it, don't end it," position continues to be the dominant policy position on affirmative action.

Years later, in March 2008, when a candidate for president, Barack Obama gave a highly regarded speech on race on the steps of Constitution Hall in Philadelphia. In that speech, he said that race

> finds voice in the church on Sunday morning, in the pulpit and in the pews. The fact that so many people are surprised to hear that anger in some of Reverend Wright's sermons simply reminds us of the old truism that the most segregated hour in American life occurs on Sunday morning. That anger is not always productive; indeed, all too often it distracts attention from solving real problems; it keeps us from squarely facing our own complicity in our condition, and prevents the African-American community from forging the alliances it needs to bring about real change. But the anger is real; it is powerful; and to simply wish it away, to condemn it without understanding its roots, only serves to widen the chasm of misunderstanding that exists between the races.

In fact, a similar anger exists within segments of the white community. Most working- and middle-class white Americans don't feel that they have been particularly privileged by their race. Their experience is the immigrant experience—as far as they're concerned, no one's handed them anything, they've built it from scratch. They've worked hard all their lives, many times only to see their jobs shipped overseas or their pension dumped after a lifetime of labor. They are anxious about their futures, and feel their dreams slipping away; in an era of stagnant wages and global competition, opportunity comes to be seen as a zero sum game, in which your dreams come at my expense. So when they are told to bus their children to a school across town; when they hear that an African American is getting an advantage in landing a good job or a spot in a good college because of an injustice that they themselves never committed; when they're told that their fears about crime in urban neighborhoods are somehow prejudiced, resentment builds over time.

Like the anger within the black community, these resentments aren't always expressed in polite company. But they have helped shape the political landscape for at least a generation. Anger over welfare and affirmative action helped forge the Reagan Coalition. Politicians routinely exploited fears of crime for their own electoral ends. Talk show hosts and conservative commentators built entire careers unmasking bogus claims of racism while dismissing legitimate discussions of racial injustice and inequality as mere political correctness or reverse racism.

Just as black anger often proved counterproductive, so have these white resentments distracted attention from the real culprits of the middle class squeeze—a corporate culture rife with inside dealing, questionable accounting practices, and short-term greed; a Washington dominated by lobbyists and special interests; economic policies that favor the few over the many. And yet, to wish away the resentments of white Americans, to label them as misguided or even racist, without recognizing they are grounded in legitimate concerns—this too widens the racial divide and blocks the path to understanding.

This is where we are right now. It's a racial stalemate we've been stuck in for years. Contrary to the claims of some of my critics, black and white, I have never been so naïve as to believe that we can get beyond our racial divisions in a single election cycle, or with a single candidacy—particularly a candidacy as imperfect as my own.

But I have asserted a firm conviction—a conviction rooted in my faith in God and my faith in the American people—that working together we can move beyond some of our old racial wounds, and that in fact we have no choice if we are to continue on the path of a more perfect union.

Although it is in far more personal and lofty terms, like President Clinton's speech, President Obama's speech is also about a balancing point between extreme positions on affirmative action.

The George W. Bush administration, sandwiched between the Clinton and Obama administrations, is most notable for the appointment of Supreme Court justices opposed to the continuation of affirmative action and opposed to "reverse discrimination." Nevertheless, the center "mend it, don't bend it," position continues to have the high ground. But it is not the position of the Bush administration on affirmative action that will be remembered, it is Hurricanes Katrina and Rita. As is often the case, it is not political ideology or policy that influences public affairs; it is events and responses to events that matter. Many factors came together to leave the country ill prepared to respond to a natural disaster such as Katrina and Rita. The Federal Emergency Management Administration (FEMA) was placed in the newly established Department of Homeland Security, distancing it from top policy-level influence. The FEMA director was not appointed based on substantive competence but based on politics. Warnings were not heeded. Planning for evacuation was poor and ill-executed. As events unraveled, it became increasingly clear that Katrina and Rita were not only natural disasters, they were social equity calamities. The images of stranded African Americans without food and water will be remembered for a very long time. And, four years later, the saga of the poorly organized, under-funded, and ill-managed governmental response to Katrina and Rita is far from over.

As the first decade of the twenty-first century draws to a close, it is once again time for the decennial census. One of the lessons from the 1990 and 2000 censuses is the increasing blurring of the races. Census surveys use "tic boxes" for census takers to mark indicating the race of respondents. It turns out that more and more people do not "fit" into one of those boxes. In 2000, 5.5 percent of respondents marked the "other" box, up from 4 percent in 1990. The boxes themselves are more than a little problematic and political. There are, for example, many kinds of Asians, and the differences between Asians are often greater than the differences between some Asians and non-Asians. And, of course, the same can be said for Hispanics and other racial or ethnic categories. In the 1990 census, persons were allowed to mark just one box. In 2000 persons could mark as many as they wish. The census is an "identity politics" battleground, interest groups representing many races and ethnicities seeking to further their interests, as they see those interests, through the census. The eminent sociologist Amatai Etzioni describes these forces as follows:

The figures for 2050 may read something like the following: 51 percent white; 14 percent multiracial; 35 percent minorities. Far from dividing the country still further, the rise of the "others," along with the fact that more and more Americans will be of mixed heritage, with divergent backgrounds, will serve to blur racial lines. That is, while there may well be more Americans of non-European origin, a growing number of the American white majority will have an Hispanic daughter- or son-in-law, an Asian stepfather or mother, and a whole rainbow of cousins. If one must find a simple image for the future of America, Tiger Woods, or Hawaii, as I see it, seems more appropriate than a view of a country in which Louis Farrakahn and his followers and the Aryan Nation are threatening one another. (2001, 6)

Amitai Etzioni argues for the inclusion in the 2010 census of a multiracial category or box in the survey. Such a category would have the potential to soften racial lines that divide Americans and render them more like economic differences. American families, he argues, believe they can move from one economic stratum to another by their labor and determination. But they cannot move from one race to another. "A major reason confrontations in America occur more often along racial lines is that color lines currently seem rigidly unchangeable" (Etzioni 2001, 7), and, of course, the election of a multiracial president in 2008 makes the point.

Ideas such as social equity evolve, influenced by events, policy, politics, and social change. And those who favor ideas such as social equity attempt to influence policy and politics, and those of us in public administration, the implementation of public policy. The interplay of events, policy, and politics with social equity has helped define the modern fields of public policy and administration. *Social Equity and Public Administration* is a contemporary description of some of the recent history of that interplay. While there is an attempt to be persuasive, it is recognized that one cannot prove social equity. Social equity is a point of view, a system of beliefs, an attitude, and, at its best, an ethic. Here we have reached for explanations of the place of fairness, justice, and equality in public policy and administration. And, we have reached for explanations of the interplay of social equity and policy, politics, and events, recognizing that the subject seldom stands still long enough to accommodate explanation. Finally, we have attempted to account for how social equity in public policy and administration came to be as it is, and to describe and defend how we think it ought to be.

References

Aaron, H.J., Bosworth, B., and Burtless, G.T. 1989. *Can America Afford to Grow Old? Paying for Social Security.* Washington, DC: Brookings Institution.

American Political Science Association. Report: Task Force on Inequality in America. 2004. "American Democracy in an Age of Rising Inequality," *PS: Perspective on Politics.* 2. no. 4 (December 2004) 651-665.

Anderson, T.H. 2004. *The Pursuit of Fairness: A History of Affirmative Action.* New York: Oxford University Press.

Argyris, C. 1966. "Some Causes of Organizational Ineffectiveness within the Department of State." Washington, DC: U.S. Government Printing Office, Center for International Systems Research, Occasional Paper No. 2 (November).

Aristotle. 1962. *Nicomachean Ethics*, trans. M. Ostwald. New York: Bobbs-Merrill.

Arrow, K. 1983. *Social Choice and Justice.* Cambridge, MA: Belknap Press.

Baier, A. 1981. "The Rights of Past and Future Persons." In *Responsibilities to Future Generations: Environmental Ethics*, ed. E. Partridge. Buffalo, NY: Prometheus.

Barry, B. 1978 "Circumstances of Justice and Future Generations." In *Obligation to Future Generations,* ed., R. Sikora and B. Barry. Philadelphia: Temple University Press.

Bartels, L.M. 2008. *Unequal Democracy: The Political Economy and the New Gilded Age.* Princeton, NJ: Princeton University Press.

Bauer, R., ed. 1967. *Social Indicators.* Cambridge, MA: MIT Press.

Baumgartner, J.S. 1963. *Project Management.* Homewood, IL: Irwin.

Bell, T.H. 1988. *The Thirteenth Man: A Reagan Cabinet Memoir.* New York: The Free Press.

Bellah, R.N., et al. 1985. *Habits of the Heart: Individualism and Commitment in American Life.* Berkeley: University of California Press.

Beremendi, P., and Anderson C. 2008. *Democracy, Inequality, and Representation.* New York: Russell Sage Foundation.

Bensen, A.A., II. 1985. "The Liability of Missouri Suburban School Districts for the Unconstitutional Segregation of Neighboring Urban School Districts." *University of Missouri at Kansas City Law Review* 53, 3: 349–75.

Black, H.C. 1957. *Black's Law Dictionary*, 4th ed. St. Paul, MN: West, 634.

Bozeman, B. 1987. *All Organizations Are Public: Bridging Public and Private Organizational Theories.* San Francisco: Jossey-Bass.

Buchanan, J.M., and Tullock, G. 1962. *The Calculus of Consent: Logical Foundations of Constitutional Democracy.* Ann Arbor: University of Michigan Press.

Burns, N. 1994. *The Formation of American Local Governments: Private Values in Public Institutions.* New York: Oxford University Press.

Callahan, D. 1981. "What Obligations Do We Have to Future Generations?" In

Responsibilities to Future Generations: Environmental Ethics, ed. E. Partridge. Buffalo, NY: Prometheus.

Carter, Dan T. 2000. *The Politics of Rage: George Wallace, the Origins of the New Conservatism, and the Transformation of American Politics,* 2nd ed. Baton Rouge, LA: Louisiana State University.

Chapman, R., and Cleaveland, F.N. 1973. "Meeting the Needs of Tomorrow's Public Service: Guidelines for Professional Education in Public Administration." Washington, DC: National Academy of Public Administration.

Chase-Dunn, C.K. 1989. *Global Formation: Structures of the World-Economy.* Cambridge, MA: Basil Blackwell.

Chitwood, S.R. 1974. "Social Equity and Social Service Productivity." *Public Administration Review* 34 (January/February): 3–51.

City of Richmond v. J.A. Croson Co. 1989. 109 S. Ct. 706.

Cleland, D.I., and King, W.R. 1968. *Systems, Organizations, Analysis, Management: A Book of Readings.* New York: McGraw-Hill.

———. 1969. *Systems Analysis and Project Management.* New York: McGraw-Hill.

Conquest, R. 2000. *Reflections on a Ravaged Century.* New York: Norton.

Considine, M., and Painter, M., eds. 1997. *Managerialism: The Great Debate.* Melbourne, Australia: Melbourne University Press.

Cuban, L., and Tyack, D. 1997. *Tinkering Toward Utopia: A Century of Public School Reform.* Cambridge, MA: Harvard University Press.

Cyert, R., and March, J. 1963. *A Behavioral Theory of the Firm.* Englewood Cliffs, NJ: Prentice-Hall.

Dalattre, E. 1972. "Rights, Responsibilities, and Future Persons." *Ethics* 82 (April): 254–58.

DeGeorge, R.T. 1979. "The Environment, Rights and Future Generations." In *Ethics and Problems of the 21st Century,* ed. K.E. Goodpaster and K.M. Sayer. Notre Dame, IN: University of Notre Dame Press.

Derr, T.S. 1981. "The Obligation to the Future." In *Responsibilities to Future Generations: Environmental Ethics,* ed. E. Partridge. Buffalo, NY: Prometheus.

Dewey, J. 1930. *Individualism, Old and New.* New York: Minton, Balch.

De tocqueville, Alexis. 2003, 1835, 1840. *Democracy in America.* New York: Penquin Classics.

Dilulio, J. 2004. "Attacking 'Sinful Inequality.'" *Perspectives on Politics.* 2, 4:661–73.

Dimock, M. 1980. *Low and Dynamic Administration.* New York: Praeger.

Downs, A. 1967. *Inside Bureaucracy.* Boston: Little, Brown.

Dworkin, R. 1985. *A Matter of Principle.* Cambridge, MA: Harvard University Press.

Etzioni, A. 1961. *A Comparative Analysis of Complex Organizations.* New York: Glencoe Free Press.

———. 2001. "The Monochrome Society." *Policy Review* 105 (March/April): 1–8.

Fayol, Henri. 1949. (original 1916). *General and Industrial Management.* trans. Constance Starrs. London: Pittman.

Fenton, J.H., and Chamberlayne, D.W. 1969. "The Literature Dealing with the Relationships Between Political Process, Socioeconomic Condition and Public Policies in the American States: A Bibliographic Essay." *Polity* (Spring): 388–404.

Finer, Herman. 1941. "Administration Responsibility in Democratic Government." *Public Administration Review* 1: 335–50.

Frederickson, H.G. 1971a. "Toward a New Public Administration." In *Toward a New Public Administration: The Minnowbrook Perspective*, ed. F. Marini. Scranton, PA: Chandler Sharp.

———. 1971b. "Organization Theory and the New Public Administration." In *Toward a New Public Administration: The Minnowbrook Perspective*, ed. F. Marini. Scranton, PA: Chandler Sharp.

———. 1971c. "Tomorrow's Organization: What Does It Mean for Public Administration?" *Public Management* 53, 7 (July): 22–26.

———, ed. 1973. *Neighborhood Control in the 1970s: Politics, Administration, and Citizen Participation.* NY: Chandler Publishing.

———, ed. 1974. "A Symposium on Social Equity and Public Administration." *Public Administration Review* 34, 1 (January/February): 1–15.

———. 1980. *New Public Administration.* University, AL: University of Alabama Press.

———. 1982. "The Recovery of Civism in Public Administration." *Public Administration Review* 42, 6 (November/December): 501–9.

———. 1990a. "Citizenship, Social Equity, and Public Administration." In *Revitalization of the Public Service*, ed. Robert B. Denhardt and Edward T. Jennings Jr. Columbia, MO: University of Missouri Press.

———. 1990b. "Public Administration and Social Equity." *Public Administration Review* 50, 2: 228–37.

———. 1997. *The Spirit of Public Administration.* San Francisco: Jossey-Bass.

———. 1999. "Ethics and the New Managerialism." *Public Integrity* 1: 265–78.

Frederickson, H.G., and Smith, K.B. 2003. *The Public Administration Theory Primer.* Boulder, CO: Westview Press.

Friedrich, C.J. 1940. "Public Policy and the Nature of Administrative Responsibility." In *Public Policy*, ed., C.J. Friedrich and F. S. Mason. Cambridge, MA: Harvard University Press.

Fullilove v. Klutznick. 1980. 448 U.S. 448.

Gilmour, R.S., and Halley, Λ.Λ., eds. 1994. *Who Makes Public Policy? The Struggle for Control Between Congress and the Executive.* Chatham, NJ: Chatham House.

Golding, M.P. 1981. "Obligations to Future Generations." In *Responsibilities to Future Generations: Environmental Ethics*, ed. E. Partridge. Buffalo, NY: Prometheus, 61–72.

Goodsell, C.T. 1983. *The Case for Bureaucracy: A Public Administration Polemic.* Chatham, NJ: Chatham House.

Goodpaster, Kenneth E. 1979. "Ethics and the Future." In *Ethics and Problems of the 21st Century*, ed. K.E. Goodpaster and K.M. Sayer. Notre Dame, IN: University of Notre Dame Press, 277–301.

Gratz v. Bollinger. 2003. 539 U.S. 244.

Green, R.M. 1981. "Intergenerational Distributive Justice and Environmental Responsibility." In *Responsibilities to Future Generations: Environmental Ethics*, ed. E. Partridge. Buffalo, NY: Prometheus.

Green v. County School Board of New Kent County. 1968. 391 U.S. 430, 437–38.

Griggs v. Duke Power Co. 1971. 401 U.S. 424.

Gruber, J.E. 1987. *Controlling Bureaucracies: Dilemmas in Democratic Governance.* Berkeley: University of California Press.

Grutter v. Bollinger. 2003. 539 U.S. 306.

Guy, M.E., ed. 1992. *Women and Men of the States: Public Administrators at the State Level*. Armonk, NY: M.E. Sharpe.

———. 1993. "Three Steps Forward, Two Steps Backward: The Status of Women's Integration into Public Management." *Public Administration Review* 53, 4: 285–92.

———. 2009. "When Diversity Makes a Difference." The Donald C. Stone Lecture, American Society for Public Administration annual conference. Miami, Florida.

Haar, C.M., and Fessler, D.W. 1986. *Fairness and Justice: Law in the Service of Equality*. New York: Simon & Schuster.

Hacker, J. 2006. *The Great Risk Shift*. New York, NY: Oxford University Press.

Hardin, G. 1980. *Promethean Ethics: Living with Death, Competition, and Triage*. Seattle: University of Washington Press.

Hargrove, E.C., and Glidewell, J.C., eds. 1990. *Impossible Jobs in Public Management*. Lawrence, KS: University Press of Kansas.

Harmon, M.M. 1989. "'Decision' and 'Action' as Contrasting Perspectives in Organization Theory." *Public Administration Review* 49, 2: 144–49.

Harmon, M.M., and Mayer, R.T. 1986. *Organization Theory for Public Administration*. Boston: Little, Brown.

Hart, D.K. 1974. "Social Equity, Justice and the Equitable Administrator." *Public Administration Review* 34 (January/February): 3–51.

Hart, D.K., and Scott, W.G. 1971. "The Moral Nature of Man in Organizations: A Comparative Analysis." *Academy of Management* 14, 2 (June): 241–55.

Hartmann, N. 1981. "Love of the Remote." In *Responsibilities to Future Generations: Environmental Ethics*, ed. E. Partridge. Buffalo, NY: Prometheus.

Hartshorne, C. 1981. "The Ethics of Contributionism." In *Responsibilities to Future Generations: Environmental Ethics*, ed. E. Partridge. Buffalo, NY: Prometheus.

Hawkins v. Town of Shaw. 1969. 303 F. Supp. 1162, 1171, N.D. MISS.

Hero, R.E. 1986. "The Urban Service Delivery Literature: Some Questions and Considerations." *Polity* 18 (Summer): 659–77.

Hirschman, A.O. 1982. *Shifting Involvements: Private Interest and Public Action*. Princeton, NJ: Princeton University Press.

———. 1991. *The Rhetoric of Reaction: Perversity, Futility, Jeopardy*. Cambridge, MA: Harvard University Press.

Hochschield, J.L. 1981. *What's Fair? American Beliefs about Distributive Justice*. Cambridge, MA: Harvard University Press.

Honey, John C. 1967. "A Report: Higher Education for Public Service." *Public Administration Review* 27 (November): 294–321.

Howard, P.K. 1995. *The Death of Common Sense: How the Law Is Suffocating America*. New York: Random House.

Hood, C., and Jackson M. 1991. *Administrative Argument*. Brookfield, VT: Dartmouth Publishing Company.

Hume, D. [1739] 1968. *Treatise of Human Nature*. New York: Oxford University Press.

Ingraham, P.W., and Rosenbloom, D.H. 1989. "The New Public Personnel and the New Public Service." *Public Administration Review* 49 (March/April): 16–24.

Jacobs, L., and Skocpol T. 2005. *Inequality and American Democracy*. New York: Russell Sage Foundation.

Jenkins v. State of Missouri. 1984a. 593 F. Supp. 1485, W.D. MO.

———. 1984b. 855 Fed. R. 8th Circuit 1297–1319.

———. 1984c. 672 F. Supp. 412.

Jonas, H. 1981. "Technology and Responsibility: The Ethics of an Endangered Future." In *Responsibilities to Future Generations: Environmental Ethics*, ed. E. Partridge. Buffalo, NY: Prometheus.

Jones, B.D., Greenberg, S.R., Kaufman, C., and Drew, J. 1978. "Service Delivery Rules and the Distribution of Local Government Services: Three Detroit Bureaucracies." *Journal of Politics* 40: 333–68.

Katz, D., and Kahn, R. 1966. *The Social Psychology of Organizations*. New York: John Wiley.

Katznelson, I. 2005. *When Affirmative Action Was White: An Untold Story of Racial Inequality in Twentieth-Century America*. New York: W.W. Norton & Co.

Kaufman, H. 1969. "Administrative Decentralization and Political Power." *Public Administration Review* 29, 1 (January–February): 3–15.

———. 1985. *Time, Chance, and Organizations: Natural Selection in a Perilous Environment*. Chatham, NJ: Chatham House.

———. 1991. *Time, Chance, and Organizations: Natural Selection in a Perilous Environment*, 2nd ed. Chatham, NJ: Chatham House.

Kavka, G. 1981. "The Futurity Problem." In *Responsibilities to Future Generations: Environmental Ethics*, ed. E. Partridge. Buffalo, NY: Prometheus.

Keister, L.A. 2000. *Wealth in America: Trends in Wealth Inequality*. Cambridge: Cambridge University Press.

Kellough, E.J. 2006. *Understanding Affirmative Action: Politics, Discrimination, and the Search for Justice*. Washington, DC: Georgetown University Press.

Kennedy, P.M. 1993. *Preparing for the Twenty-first Century*. New York: Random House.

Kettl, D.F. 1993. *Sharing Power: Public Governance and Private Markets*. Washington, DC: Brookings Institution.

Koppell, J. 2003. *The Politics of Quasi-Government Hybrid Organizations and the Dynamics of Bureaucratic Control*. Cambridge, MA: Cambridge University Press.

Koppell, J. Forthcoming. *World Rule: The Politics of Global Governance*. Chicago: University of Chicago Press.

Kotlikoff, L.J. 1992. *Generational Accounting: Knowing Who Pays, and When, for What We Spend*. New York: Free Press.

Krislov, S. 1974. *Representative Bureaucracy*. Englewood Cliffs, NJ: Prentice Hall.

Kuhn, T. 1970. *Structure of Scientific Revolutions*, 2nd ed. Chicago: University of Chicago Press.

Lasch, C. 1978. *The Culture of Narcissism: American Life in an Age of Diminishing Expectations*. New York: Norton.

———. 1990. *The True and Only Heaven: Progress and Its Critics*. New York: Norton.

Levy, F. 1987. *Dollars and Dreams: The Changing American Income Distribution*. New York: Russell Sage Foundation.

Liddell v. State of Missouri. 1984. 731 F. 2D 1294, 1323, 8 Cir.

Light, P. 1995. *Thickening Government: Federal Hierarchy and the Diffusion of Accountability*. Washington, DC: Brookings Institution.

———. 1999. *The True Size of Government*. Washington, DC: Brookings Institution.

Likert, R. 1961. *New Patterns of Management*. New York: McGraw-Hill.

———. 1967. *The Human Organization: Its Management and Value*. New York: McGraw-Hill.

Lindbloom, C.E. 1965. *The Intelligence of Democracy: Decision Making through Mutual Adjustment*. New York: Free Press.

Lineberry, R.L. 1977. *Equality and Urban Policy: The Distribution of Municipal Public Services*. Thousand Oaks, CA: Sage.

Link, A.S. 1971. *The Higher Realism of Woodrow Wilson, and Other Essays*. Nashville, TN.: Vanderbilt University Press.

Locke, J. [1690] 1967. *Two Treatises of Government*, 2nd ed., ed. Peter Laslett. New York: Cambridge University Press.

Lowi, T.J. 1969. *The End of Liberalism: Ideology, Policy, and the Crisis of Public Authority*. New York: Norton.

March, J.G., and Simon, H.A. 1963. *Organizations*. New York: Wiley.

Marini, F., ed. 1971. *Toward a New Public Administration: The Minnowbrook Perspective*. Scranton, PA: Chandler Sharp.

Maynard-Moody, S., and Musheno M. 2003. *Cops, Teachers, Counselors: Stories from the Front Lines of Public Service*. Ann Arbor: University of Michigan Press.

McCarty, N., Poole, K.T., and Rosenthal, H. 2008. *Polarized America: Dance of Ideology and Unequal Riches*. Cambridge, MA: MIT Press.

McKerlie, D. 1989. "Equality and Time." *Ethics* 99, 3 (April): 475–91.

Mead, L.M. 2004. "The Great Passivity." *Perspectives on Politics* 2, 4: 671–75.

Meier, K.J. 1993. "Representative Bureaucracy: A Theoretical and Empirical Exposition." In *Research in Public Administration*, vol. 2, ed. James L. Perry. Greenwich, CT: JAI Press, 1–35.

Meier, K.J., and Smith, K.B. 1994. "Representative Democracy and Representative Bureaucracy: Examining the Top-Down and Bottom-Up Linkages." *Social Science Quarterly* 75, 4: 790–803.

Meier, K.J., Wrinkle, R.D., and Polinard, J.L. 1999. "Representative Bureaucracy and Distributional Equity: Addressing the Hard Question." *Journal of Politics* 61, 4: 1025–39.

State of Missouri v. Jenkins. 1995. 115 S. Ct. 2573, June 14.

Mosher, F.C., ed. 1967. *Governmental Reorganizations: Cases and Commentary*. Indianapolis: Bobbs-Merrill.

Naff, K.C. 2001. *To Look Like America: Dismantling Barriers for Women and Minorities in Government*. Boulder, CO: Westview Press.

Nalbandian, J. 1989. "The U.S. Supreme Court's 'Consensus' on Affirmative Action." *Public Administration Review* 49, 1 (January/February): 38–45.

———. 1991. *Professionalism in Local Government: Transformations in the Roles, Responsibilities, and Values of City Managers*. San Francisco: Jossey-Bass.

Neustadt, R.E., and May, E.R. 1986. *Thinking in Time: The Uses of History for Decision-Makers*. New York: Free Press.

Nemerov, Howard. 1987. "Ultima Ratio Reagan." In *War Stories: Poems of Long Ago and Now*. Chicago: University of Chicago Press, p. 6.

Niskanen, W.K. 1971. *A Bureaucracy and Representative Government*. Hawthorne, NY: Aldine de Gruyter.

O'Leary, R. 2006. *The Ethics of Dissent: Managing Guerrilla Government*. Washington, DC: Congressional Quarterly Press.

Osborne, D., and Gaebler, T. 1992. *Reinventing Government: How the Entrepreneurial Spirit Is Transforming the Public Sector*. Reading, MA: Addison-Wesley.

Ostrom, V. 1973. *The Intellectual Crisis in American Public Administration*. University, AL: University of Alabama Press.

Page, B. 1983. *Who Gets What from Government*. Berkeley: University of California Press.

Page, B., and Jacobs L.K. 2009. *Class War? What Americans Really Think About Inequality*. Chicago: University of Chicago Press.

Page, S.E. 2007. *The Difference: How the Power of Diversity Creates Better Groups, Firms, Schools, and Societies*. Princeton, NJ: Princeton University Press.

Palmer, P.J. 1981. *The Company of Strangers*. New York: Crossroads.

Parfit, D. 1984. *Reason and Persons*. Oxford, England: Claredon Press.

Partridge, E. 1981. "Who Cares About the Future." In *Responsibilities to Future Generations: Environmental Ethics*, ed. E. Partridge. Buffalo, NY: Prometheus.

Perrow, C. 1972. "The New Public Administration." *Public Management* 32, 6 (November/December): 66–79.

Phillips, K. 2003. *Wealth and Democracy: A Political History of the American Rich*. New York: Broadway Books.

Plato. 1970. *The Laws*, trans. T.J. Saunders. New York: Penguin Books.

Pletcher, Galen R. 1981. "The Rights of Future Generations." In *Responsibilities to Future Generations: Environmental Ethics*, ed. E. Partridge. Buffalo, NY: Prometheus, 167–70.

Presthus, Robert. 1962. *The Organizational Society*. New York: Alfred A. Knopf.

Price, J.L. 1968. *Organizational Effectiveness*. Homewood, IL: Irwin.

Putnam, R.D., Leonardi R., and Nanetti R.U. 1993. *Making Democracy Work: Civic Traditions in Modern Italy*. Princeton, NJ: Princeton University Press.

Rae, D., and Yates, D., et al. 1981. *Equalities*. Cambridge, MA: Harvard University Press.

Rawls, J.A. 1971. *A Theory of Justice*. Cambridge, MA: Belknap Press.

Regents of the University of California v. Bakke. 1978. 438 U.S. 265.

Report to the President (William J. Clinton). 1995. "Affirmative Action Review." U.S. Archives.

Ricci et al. v. DeStefano. 2009. 07-1428, 08-328.

Riccucci, N.M. 2002. *Managing Diversity in Public Sector Workforces*. Boulder, CO: Westview Press.

———. 2009. "The Pursuit of Social Equity in the Federal Government: A Road Less Traveled." *Public Administration Review* 69, 3 (May/June): 373–86.

Rice, M.F., ed. 2005. *Diversity and Public Administration: Theory, Issues, and Perspectives*. Armonk, NY: M.E. Sharpe.

Roberts, J.M. 1999. *Twentieth Century: The History of the World, 1901–2000*. New York: Viking.

Rohr, J.A. 1989. *Ethics for Bureaucrats: An Essay on Law and Virtue*, 2nd ed. New York: Dekker.

Rosenbloom, D.H. 1977. *Federal Equal Employment Opportunity: Politics and Public Personnel Administration*. New York: Praeger.

———. 1983. *Public Administration and Law: Bench v. Bureau in the United States*. New York: Dekker.

Rourke, F.E. 1976. *Bureaucracy, Politics, and Public Policy*, 2nd ed. Boston: Little, Brown.

Schlesinger, A.M. 1986. *The Cycles of American History*. Boston: Houghton Mifflin.

Scharr, J. 1964. "Some Ways of Thinking About Equality." *Journal of Politics* 26: 862–95.

————. 1967. "Equal Opportunity and Beyond." In *INOMOS IX=Equality*, R. Pennock and J.W. Chapman, ed. New York: Atherton. 226–52.

Schultze, C.L. 1969. *The Politics and Economics of Public Spending*. Washington, DC: Brookings Institution.

Selden, S.C. 2006. "A Solution in Search of a Problem? Discrimination, Affirmative Action, and the New Public Service." *Public Administration Review* 60, 6 (November/December): 911–23.

John Serrano Jr. et al. v. Ivy Baker Priest. 1978. 5 Cal. 3d 584.

Shafritz, J.M., and Russell, E.W. 2000. *Introducing Public Administration*, 2nd ed. New York: Longman.

Simon, H.A. 1946. "The Proverbs of Administration." *Public Administration Review* 6: 53–67.

————. 1957. *Administrative Behavior*, 2nd ed. New York: McMillan.

————. 1960. *The New Science of Management Decision*. New York: Harper-Collins.

————. 1998. "Designing Organizations for an Information Rich World." In *Models of Bounded Rationality*, vol. 2. Cambridge, MA: MIT Press.

Smith, T.A. 1988. *Time and Public Policy*. Knoxville: University of Tennessee Press.

Steiner, G.A., and Ryan, W.G. 1968. *Industrial Project Management*. New York: MacMillan.

Stern, Phillip Van Doren, ed. 1940. *The Life and Writings of Abraham Lincoln*. New York: Random House.

Stiefel, L., and Berne, R. 1981. "The Equity Effects of State School Finance Reform: A Methodological Critique and New Evidence." *Policy Sciences* 13, 1: 75–98.

Strange, S. 1988. *States and Markets*. London: Pinter.

————. 1996. *The Retreat of the State: The Diffusion of Power in the World Economy*. Cambridge: Cambridge University Press.

Strauss, W., and Howe, N. 1991. *Generations: The History of America's Future, 1584–2069*. New York: Morrow.

Swann v. Charlotte-Mecklenburg Board of Education. 1971. 402 U.S. 1.

Taylor, F.W. 1985. *The Principles of Scientific Management*. Easton, PA: Hive.

Thompson, J.D. 1967. *Organizations in Action: Social Science Bases of Administrative Theory*. New York: McGraw-Hill.

Thompson, V.A. 1961. *Modern Organization*. New York: Alfred A. Knopf.

————. 1975. *Without Sympathy or Enthusiasm: The Problem of Administrative Compassion*. University, AL: University of Alabama Press.

Tuchman, B.W. 1984. *The March of Folly: From Troy to Vietnam*. New York: Ballantine.

Tullock, G. 1965. *The Politics of Bureaucracy*. Washington, DC: Public Affairs Press.

United States v. Jefferson County Board of Eduction. 1972. 466 F.2d. 1213.

University of California Regents v. Bakke. 1978. 438 v. s 265.B

Waldo, D. 1948. *The Administrative State: A Study of the Political Theory of American Public Administration*. New York: Ronald Press.

————. 1968. "Scope of the Theory of Public Administration." In *Theory and Practice of Public Administration: Scope, Objectives and Methods*, ed. J.C. Charlesworth. Philadelphia, PA: The American Academy of Political and Social Sciences, 1–26.

———, ed. 1971. *Public Administration in a Time of Turbulence*. San Francisco: Chandler.

———. 1972. "Development in Public Administration." *The Annals of the American Academy of Political and Social Science*: 404, 224.

———. 1974. "Symposium on Social Equity and Public Administration." *Public Administration Review* 34 (January/February).

———. 1990. "A Theory of Public Administration Means in Our Time a Theory of Politics Also." In *Public Administration: The State of the Discipline*, ed. N.B. Lynn and A. Wildavsky. Chatham, NJ: Chatham House.

Walster, E., and Walster, G.W. 1975. "Equity and Social Justice." *Journal of Social Issues* 31, 3: 2–43.

Walzer, M. 1983. *Spheres of Justice: A Defense of Pluralism and Equality*. New York: Basic Books.

Warren, M.A. 1981. "Do Potential Persons Have Rights?" In *Responsibilities to Future Generations: Environmental Ethics*, ed. E. Partridge. Buffalo, NY: Prometheus.

Weir, Margaret. 2004." Challenging Inequality," *PS: Perspective in Politics* 2. no. 4 (December): 677-685.

White, O. 1969. "The Dialectical Organization: An Alternative to Bureaucracy." *Public Administration Review* 29, 1 (January–February): 32–42.

Whitehead, B.D. 1993. "Dan Quayle Was Right." *The Atlantic Monthly* 271, 4 (April): 47–84.

Wilcox, H. 1968. "The Cultural Traits of Hierarchy in Middle Class Children." *Public Administration Review* 29, 2 (March/April): 222–35.

Wildavsky, A. 1964. *The Politics of the Budgetary Process*. Boston, MA: Little, Brown.

———. 1988. "Ubiquitous Anomie: Public Service in an Era of Ideological Dissensus." *Public Administration Review* 48, 4: 753–55.

Wilensky, P. 1981. "Efficiency or Equity: Competing Values in Administrative Reform." *Policy Studies Journal* 9, 1239–49.

Will, G. 2009. "Case May Unravel Racial Spoils System." *Lawrence Journal World* (April 27): 7A.

Willbern, Y. 1973. "Is the New Public Administration Still with Us?" *Public Administration Review* 33, 4 (July/August): 376.

Wilson, J.Q. 1989. *Bureaucracy: What Government Agencies Do and Why They Do It*. New York: Basic Books.

———. 1993. "The Moral Sense." *American Political Science Review* 83, 1: 1–10.

Wilson, W. [1887] 1941. "The Study of Administration." *Political Science Quarterly* 56, 2 (December): 197–222.

Wilson, W.J. 1987. *The Truly Disadvantaged: The Inner City, the Underclass, and Public Policy*. Chicago: The University of Chicago Press.

———. 2009. *More than Just Race: Being Black and Poor in the Inner City*. New York: W.W. Norton & Co.

Wise, L.R. 1990. "Social Equity in Civil Service Systems." *Public Administration Review* 50, 5: 567–75.

World Commission on Environment and Development. 1987. *Our Common Future*. Oxford: Oxford University Press.

Wright, D.S. 1968. *Federal Grants-In-Aid: Perspectives and Alternatives*. Washington, DC: American Enterprise Institute for Public Policy Research.

Yankelovich, D. 1994. "How Changes in the Economy Are Reshaping American Values." In *Values and Public Policy*, ed. H.J. Aaron, T.E. Mann, and T. Taylor. Washington, DC: Brookings Institution.

Yergin, D., and Stanislaw, J. 1998. *The Commanding Heights: The Battle between Government and the Marketplace that Is Remaking the Modern World.* New York: Simon and Schuster.

Index

About the Author

H. George Frederickson is the Edwin O. Stene Distinguished Professor of Public Administration at the University of Kansas. In 2003–2004 he served as the Winant Visiting Professor of American Government at the University of Oxford, and as a Fellow of Balliol College, Oxford. He is a co-author of *The Public Administration Theory Primer* (with Kevin B. Smith 2003); *The Adapted City: Institutional Dynamics and Structural Change* (with Gary A. Johnson and Curtis H. Wood 2004); and *Measuring the Performance of the Hollow State* (with David G. Frederickson 2006). He has received the John Gaus Award, the Donald Stone Lecturer Award, the Dwight Waldo Award, and the Distinguished Research Award. The Public Management Research Association has named its career contributions to research award in his honor.